DISRUPTING RELIGION

Exposing Deceptions and Unveiling Mysteries
to Release God's Sons and Daughters

COLIN FERREIRA

I dedicate this book to my nine children, Seth, Benjamin, Melody, Regan, Caleb, Jesse, Jedd, Raanan, and Samuel. It is my deepest desire that you will look past my flawed representation of a father and find your ultimate Father. I love you all so much!

Contents

INTRODUCTION

We are in a season of severe shaking—a season of disruption! We are experiencing things at a global level that no one would have expected. Almost every day, we see and hear the unimaginable. There is a phrase that is becoming common during this season: *You couldn't make this up!*

I began writing this book on Friday, March 13, 2020, the very day President Donald J. Trump declared a National State of Emergency here in the United States in response to the fast-spreading coronavirus known as COVID-19.

Throughout the course of this writing, other social upheavals have been unfolding with protests, rioting, and anarchy taking place in various cities. Anger and fear appear to be rampant everywhere! The pandemic and the response to it have disrupted people's lives across the globe. Financial markets have experienced volatility not seen since 1929. An enormous amount of wealth has evaporated, and countless businesses either have already gone under or at risk of doing so. Tens of millions of workers have been furloughed or lost their jobs entirely. We have been instructed to *social distance,* as many states have locked down completely. We were later told that scientific models were wrong and the numbers of deaths from the virus were skewed. In short, we have been receiving mixed messages from the media and government authorities at many levels. It's hard to know who to trust.

As if this is not enough, here in the United States, we are probably entering into a time of political and social upheaval like nothing this generation has seen before arising out of a critical presidential election on the horizon. The future is extremely unpredictable.

In short, Everything that can be shaken seems to be shaking. As Stephen Covey said, one of the few constants is change.

As this has been unfolding, many churches have also been locked down. Christians have not been able to gather as they used to on a weekly basis. We have been given little choice but to reevaluate our spiritual lives and the thing we call *Church*. The unfolding events and the reactions to them reveal that we are at significant crossroads within both the global political arena and the Church.

For decades, there have been consistent efforts to dismantle our Judeo-Christian culture in order to replace our individual and national freedoms with what many call *globalization*—a one-world order of godless state control or statism. These are not just inconsequential random events degrading our societies, but an intentional agenda that has been unfolding over many years with the goal of replacing God, and our dependence on Him, with man's own power expressed in the State. This dismantling of our values has been happening at an alarming rate because we have allowed the secular world to control the key areas of cultural influence: government, courts, education, media, arts and entertainment, business, family, and even religion.

The majority of Americans—and a third of the world—claim to be believers, and yet we have been losing significant ground for the last few generations. While most hate to admit it, we feel powerless to change it. We have been given the mandate to take dominion over the earth, but for quite some time, God's Kingdom and rule seem to be shrinking instead of expanding. Sadly, while we seem to accept basic doctrines, we do not walk in our true identity or exercise faith in God's ability or His desire to do anything meaningful about this disturbing trend. Like the Scriptures say, we have a form of godliness but we deny the power thereof. (2 Timothy 3:5 NKJV)

Is this a book of doom and gloom? Certainly not. It is quite the opposite. I have a strong sense of positive anticipation because I know God is working this all for good in significant ways. I began this introduction the way I did because, in order to appreciate what is happening in the spirit realm, we need to acknowledge that the world has been heading in the wrong direction for decades. And let's face it, what the Church has been doing is, to put it mildly, not working well.

With the recent disruptions and lockdowns, God has placed His Church in a pit stop. Pit stops are used in car racing to pull a vehicle out of a race (off of its course) temporarily to effectively equip it for what still lies ahead. Without pit stops, the vehicle has no hope of achieving victory. Pit stops involve refueling, changing tires, making mechanical adjustments or even major repairs, and giving the driver instructions and a few moments of rest. However, this pit stop God has placed the Church in now is far more than for a quick refueling and new tires! This is more like an extreme makeover! I say this because the vehicle presently in this race will never see victory without a dramatic reformation.

This book is about just that—reforming His Church through a major paradigm shift. I am certain that we have just entered a season of deep change within the Church. This is not a period of tweaking and adding a new coat of paint. It's not about embracing modern technology to continue doing the same thing. It's about tearing down and rebuilding, a time where nothing is off-limits. It is about the Father connecting with His children in a way they have never experienced before.

No one likes pit stops because it requires a willingness to leave the crowd, to give up one's position in the race, and allow everyone else seemingly to get ahead. After this pit stop, however, it is my belief that the Church will re-enter the race very differently from how it left. It will be far more powerful and well equipped for victory—and the reformation has already begun.

A surge of hope is pouring out of many prophets today in the midst of evil and madness. Even as blatant evil unfolds before our eyes, God is moving in this particular time in history to bring about the greatest revival ever and through His Church—His Body. I am certain one of the prerequisites to this revival is a personal reformation in the minds and hearts of believers. Our thinking guides our faith and our actions. We cannot continue to think like we have been and expect to see meaningful change. Reformation must precede the coming revival.

I have not been given the mandate to speak to many of the facets of what God is doing today in this significant time. My focus is on a core set of issues and beliefs within the Church that clearly need to be addressed *now*! It is my hope that you will see with fresh eyes that there is a Gospel filled with mysteries that further unlock our hearts and release us to usher in the greatest revival of all time.

But to do that, God is disrupting religion.

"Behold, I will do a new thing, Now it shall spring forth; shall you not know it?" (Isaiah 43:19a NKJV)

Section One

WHERE ARE WE?

Chapter 1

HOW ON EARTH DID WE GET HERE?

I am Trinidadian by birth. I have been living in the United States of America with my wife and nine children since April 2006 and am now a citizen of this amazing country.

As a person who lived in a developing country for the first forty-nine years of my life, I had the deepest respect for the United States. I will never forget the thrill I felt when, with my eyes glued to the TV, I watched the opening ceremony of the 1984 Summer Olympics in Los Angeles. Neil Diamond sang his hit song *America,* and fighter jets did a low flyover. I would have done anything at the time to call myself an American.

When I finally did move to America, however, I began seeing signs of cracks in the nation's foundations that most Americans just could not see. They had bought into the belief that America will always be the greatest country on Earth—no matter what.

What I had not realized was the magnitude of the enemy's long-term strategy to control key culture influencers, particularly our education system, the media, government, courts, and the arts and entertainment industry. It seemed to me as if a growing colony of termites had been eating the foundation of a magnificent building for decades. These termites have been multiplying at an alarming rate, moving up into the higher levels of the building and every room. In the past, their destructive activity was invisible to most, but lately, a simple poke with the finger punctures what used to be a solid structure to reveal the destruction within.

It seemed to me as if a growing colony of termites had been eating the foundation of a magnificent building for decades.

For example, never in my wildest dreams would I think America would have same-sex marriage, or illegal immigrants would be given more rights and protection than citizens. Never in my wildest imagination would I think socialism would be even considered by a sizable portion of the population of this nation, or biological men would be allowed to compete in a woman's sport by merely self-identifying as a woman.

Worst of all, over 60 million babies have been killed since abortion was legalized. In some states now, a full-term baby can be legally murdered just before birth, but destroying a bald eagle's egg brings a strong penalty. These are just a few examples of previously unthinkable developments we have now accepted into our society. These developments are beyond my comprehension. The framers of our Constitution never clarified these issues specifically because such issues were simply unthinkable to them.

One thing is not debatable: the Church is not functioning in the power and authority given to it. From the days of Adam, we have been placed on the earth to walk in close fellowship with God and take dominion over the earth. We all know well what Adam and Eve caused, but Jesus was sent to reverse it all—to save mankind, to restore our relationship to the Father, and restore our authority over the earth. He wants to build His Kingdom rule here *as it is in heaven.*

The early Church started well, but a lot has changed since then. Presently, instead of being the counterculture we were intended to be, we have become a subculture, operating under and controlled by the growing secular culture. The stark truth is the Church has become the tail being wagged and not the head leading the way.

Yet the simple arithmetic just does not add up! Over two billion people in the world claim to be Christians. They are supposed to be filled with the same Spirit who raised Christ from the dead, yet we are struggling, at best, in this battle for our nation and world.

When referring to the miracles He performed, Jesus said, "Greater things you will do." So why are we not experiencing these *greater things* today? How could our nation be saturated with Christian churches while our culture and values are pulled out from under us? The Bible says that whatsoever we ask in His name, we will have it. But is that what the vast majority of Christians experience?

> *The stark truth is the Church has become the tail being wagged and not the head leading the way.*

Even from these few questions, our answers indicate something is clearly wrong. There is a disconnect, and we all know it. Do we really believe that God intended this to be our experience? I do not think so.

Unfortunately, when we say we believe everything God says is true—and still feel that disconnect—then we each personally conclude, *Something must be wrong with me.* I, for one, felt for many years that I must be exceptionally broken, even as a Christian. The answers always seemed to elude me, like a butterfly flitting away just beyond my grasp.

Now I am not claiming to have *the* answer, as I believe there are a number of issues that bring us to where we are today. However, I do feel strongly that God has given me clarity about some significant pieces of this puzzle.

God is moving right now in critical ways to bring about needed reformation within the Church. We are at a significant and historic period in biblical history. The Church is being given the opportunity not to reset, but to reform. This is not a time for tweaking and adjusting, or for going back to what existed—even if parts of it were good. We are in a time of metamorphosis. For example, we should not be seeking to return to the early church days. Jesus is returning for a mature Church that has grown up.

LIKE A CHILD

Just prior to beginning to write this book, I moved to Georgia, USA, after experiencing an intense wilderness-like experience in Iowa. The journey had led me from my birth country, Trinidad, to my wife's hometown, a little religious community in Iowa. During that experience in rural Iowa, which lasted over twelve years, everything drastically changed for me. After the initial excitement of the move had worn off, I began to feel lost and without purpose. My business was and is still in Trinidad, so I do not leave the house to work. Because we also homeschool our children, I began feeling like I was under house arrest.

The most challenging and unexpected change for me was the loss of my identity as I knew it. In Trinidad, I had been the CEO and owner of a leading optical business, a church elder, president of the Christian Chamber of Commerce, and leading marketplace ministry on a national level.

I walked away from it all at a time when it was all going very well (I will explain more later). However, I was not prepared for what followed. As the years passed in Iowa, I felt a growing sense of deep loss. I struggled with periods of depression and hopelessness like I never felt before. I often wondered if my purpose and destiny had been shipwrecked, although my heart towards God had not changed. I was not wired for the culture or climate of rural Iowa, and certainly not prepared for the loss of purpose and my perceived value. My only hope was in prophetic words I had received years earlier (another story I'll share later), but even those words contradicted everything I was experiencing.

About four years into this difficult time, God used a young man at a conference to speak into my life. Within ten minutes of talking with him, he revealed I was struggling with an identity crisis. He told me God had separated me completely from my former identity so He could reveal to me my true identity. In a deep, heartfelt way, I suddenly realized all that really matters is that I am *His beloved son*. I cannot fully express the emotions I felt at the time. The experience was as profound as the day I was born again.

We all claim to understand that we are God's children. However, much of modern western Christianity sees this as a position rather than a specific, ongoing, engaging relationship with Father God.

Apparently, I had to die to everything I initially considered to be my identity so I could see more clearly something I really thought I already knew. That day I recalled the meaning of my name, a meaning I never cared for as a boy. But that day, it meant everything to me. In Gaelic, my name *Colin* means *child*.

Over time, I came to realize that the Church is filled with servants of the Lord, but very few who truly act like His sons and daughters. We all claim to understand that we are God's children. However, much of modern western Christianity sees this as a position rather than a specific, ongoing, engaging relationship with Father God. Too many of us see it like receiving new citizenship to another nation or having our last name changed. It is perceived as something officially or technically true, while engaging with our heavenly Father all day, every day, as a kid in a healthy home environment seems foreign to us.

As a matter of fact, most of us are not clear on how exactly to relate with the Father because we have been taught primarily about our relationship with Jesus. We have lost sight of the fact that it was the Father who sent Jesus to restore us to an intimate relationship with Him. We all claim to know that the Father wants us to be *like Jesus*, but what does that really mean? Religion says it is all about character— doing the right things—but that is not true. The Father wants us to walk in relationship with Him *just like Jesus did*. He wants us to fully understand our identity in Him and enjoy the same complete confidence Jesus enjoyed. And He wants us to have the complete faith that comes from engaging in this relationship with Him—just like Jesus demonstrated.

The chief reason the Christian Church today is so weak is this: we misunderstand the true nature of our relationship with the Father.

As we sought to name our nine children, we looked for names that had a positive meaning because we believe names can have a prophetic element that speaks into one's life. I often wondered, what was the prophetic element to my name? As I pondered this, the Lord brought to mind the name *Elijah*, which in Hebrew means, *My God is Yahweh* or *the Lord is God*. At first, I wondered how that phrase could have anything to do with Elijah's destiny. Then I realized what Elijah's ultimate challenge on Mt. Carmel was all about. (1 Kings 18) He revealed to all Israel in a profound way that the true God *is Yahweh*— the Lord *is* God.

Through those difficult years in the Iowa *wilderness*, I developed a strong passion to help the Church understand the significance of living in our true identity as children of God. This passion within me is like what Jeremiah described: "His word was in my heart like a burning fire shut up in my bones; I was weary holding it back, And I could not." (Jeremiah 20:9 NKJV)

CHAIN MAIL DISTORTIONS

In this book, I'll be unraveling a number of distortions prevalent throughout modern Christianity. I pray they will shift how you see God, yourself, and the Good News in significant ways that affect your experience as a Christian and increase your peace, faith, and authority. If your experience is anything like mine, you will probably wonder why you could not see these distortions before! The answer is simple: forces of darkness and deception have infiltrated the Church for centuries to form what I describe as *chain mail*.

Chain mail is a form of armor developed in the Middle Ages. It is made of small metal rings firmly linked together to form a strong garment-like protection for a knight's vital organs. Yet Satan has flipped this image to weave distortions like chain mail around the hearts of believers. Instead of keeping threats out, these distortions have combined over time to block truth and cut us off from truly understanding the love of our Father. It is my hope that the truth I share will destroy enough of these rings of lies to dismantle this chain mail and allow the sword of Spirit, the word of God, to reach our hearts in new ways.

This chain mail analogy also suggests another reason we struggle to receive truth: we're not open to receive the mysteries of God. God intentionally allowed many truths to be hidden in mysteries *unless* our hearts are truly open to receive and understand them at all costs. The ability to see truth transcends positions, titles, academic achievements (even religious ones), and all other benchmarks assumed by worldly thinking. This reality is so important that I will be focusing specifically on it in chapter 4, but Jesus' choice of the twelve apostles is one undisputed example.

As we come to see the deception of the enemy and begin to understand more of God's hidden mysteries, I pray it will begin a chain reaction of new revelation that continues long after you have read this book. I am also confident that this chain reaction will cause faith to increase and the world to see a manifestation of God's love and power like never before through the revealing of His true sons and daughters. "For the earnest expectation of the creation eagerly waits for the revealing of the sons of God...because the creation itself also will be delivered from the bondage of corruption into the glorious liberty of the children of God." (Romans 8:19-21 NKJV)

THE PROBLEM AS JESUS DESCRIBED IT

Jesus best explained the problem we face in the parable of the prodigal son found in the Gospel of Luke. (Chapter 15:11-32) There is a lot to discuss in the story, some of which I will revisit later, but to put the parable in proper context, we need to read the entire chapter.

The chapter begins with the reason why Jesus gave the three parables we often refer to as The Lost Sheep, The Lost Coin, and The Lost Son. The Pharisees and other teachers of religious law were complaining because Jesus was associating with tax collectors and other rejects of Jewish society. The parables, particularly the last one, were Jesus' direct response to their complaints. Each of the parables is similar in that what was lost was precious to someone and worth every effort to retrieve.

However, the last parable introduced another significant dimension which made it stand out from the others—the elder son. Giving three similar parables, but with a unique addition to the last one, caused the added piece about the elder son to become Jesus' focal point. It is the elder son who best reveals the religious mindset of the Pharisees that each of us still wrestles with today.

The elder son represents the vast majority of the Church throughout the centuries. Bear in mind, he *was a son* (parallel to any born-again child of God), already a member of the father's household. He was not a servant. All that the father had was his, but he drove himself anyway to slave in his father's fields to earn or deserve his inheritance. With all his long hours slaving in the fields, he probably spent very little time developing a healthy active relationship with his father.

For had he been close to his father, he would have learned slaving was not what pleased his father. Working harder was not what earned his father's love, blessing, or inheritance. Had he been intimate with his father, he would have expected his father to respond exactly as he did when his brother returned home. Had he truly understood his own identity as a child of his father, he would have genuinely joined his father in celebrating the restoration of his brother. He might even have gone to look for his brother to bring him back to the father, as Jesus did for us.

This subconscious avoidance of true relationship with the Father is one of the main causes why the modern Church is so weak, and why our culture has declined. We judge our spirituality and whether we are deserving of blessing by what we do for God.

One of the biggest mistakes we tend to make when reading about the Pharisees and other religious leaders of that time is to think of them as an evil religious sect that persecuted Jesus, and yet fail to see our own similar tendencies. However, their stories were recorded through the intentional inspiration of the Holy Spirit to reveal how easy it is to live religious lives focused on performance rather than enjoying genuine relationships with our Father.

This subconscious avoidance of true relationship with the Father is one of the main causes why the modern Church is so weak, and why our culture has declined. We judge our spirituality and whether we are deserving of blessing by what we *do* for God.

At this point, you may be nodding as you read, thinking what I have stated is pretty obvious. But what I have just explained is a lot more difficult to discern as we go about our daily lives, and it is having a tremendous influence on what we know as "church" today. A lot more will be said on this further on in this book.

A TIME OF REFORMATION

From man's fall beginning with Adam, humanity lived in a general state of lawlessness and sin, not clearly knowing specifics of right from wrong until the Law was given to the Israelites through Moses. With a keener knowledge of right and wrong, they tried to do better but without success. They became stuck in a constant cycle of conviction, failure, and condemnation. God brought them to that place to reveal their need for redemption. God's promise of a redeemer was their only hope. Eventually, God sent Jesus the Redeemer to provide full restoration *purely by grace through faith* and to give all who believed the amazing privileges of becoming His sons and daughters.

This broader reality parallels my own personal experience in an unexpected way. Until I accepted Jesus, I was living a life of lawlessness and sin without much conviction. After receiving Christ, I had a deep desire to know God, read the Word, and attend church. But as I read the Word and attended church, a lot of my sin was exposed—but without proper teaching and understanding of the full extent of grace and my identity in Christ.

This absence of clarity resulted in decades of mixing faith with works, seeking to please God by better effort, and building my identity through the ministry I did for God. My life, even as a Christian who was born-again and given full access to grace, often looked more like that of the frustrated Israelites after they received the Law. As I read the Word and listened to messages in church, I was convicted to *do* better, but I did not understand how to fully rely on faith and grace to bear the fruit of the Spirit. It was not easy to see this error at the time because there was always some truth mixed in with it. There were a lot of successes in the midst of it all, but they often came at an unnecessary cost and probably still did not achieve the levels God intended. Sadly, I see various measures of this same *old covenant* behavior with most Christians today.

God is moving once again within the Church now to bring a simple yet deeper revelation of our true identity as His children in order to bring about the revealing of the sons and daughters of God—the mature Church.

I have been hearing the words *reformation* and *revival* bantered about a lot lately. The resurgence of those terms is especially interesting to me because seven years ago, when God was reprogramming my understanding, I told my wife with excitement, "This is all about reformation!"

What I will be sharing with you in the pages to follow has the potential to shift our thinking similar to the Reformation triggered by

Martin Luther in the 1500s—*seriously!* That reformation was based primarily on one simple but profound revelation that we are saved *only* by faith in Jesus Christ and not by good works.

God is moving once again within the Church now to bring a simple yet deeper revelation of our true identity as His children in order to bring about the revealing of the sons and daughters of God—the mature Church. Revival will take place to the extent that this reformation of understanding takes root in the hearts of God's people. When we experience it, we will begin functioning from a much greater level of rest, confidence, and faith as our perspective shifts from *servants* to *sons and daughters.*

If we must strive, let us not strive to gain acceptance from our Father, but rather let us strive to enter into true sonship and rest and remain there. But as the writer of Hebrews noted, that may take far more intentional effort than we realize: "Therefore, since a promise remains of entering His rest, let us fear lest any of you seem to have come short of it." (Hebrews 4:1 NKJV)

The intensity of present events and the manifestation of evil is placing America, the Church, and even the world at a crossroads. It is no longer business as usual. Everything is being shaken, and the shaking is forcing believers to stop and face the issues, not only on a natural level, but even more so on a spiritual level.

We simply cannot continue as we did and expect different results. However, moving forward effectively requires a retooling, a transformation of our minds, replacing Satan's chain mail of religious lies with a greater and clearer understanding of truth that we have just not seen before.

God in His wisdom has intentionally placed a lot of this truth in the form of mysteries that He reveals to His children under the right conditions. But before I get deeper into some of these mysteries as well as some of the enemy's carefully-crafted deceptions, I think it will help you to hear more of my own journey which led me to what I am about to share.

Chapter 2

A LEAP OVERBOARD

I am a very practical person, so anything I get involved in has to be relevant, practical, and attainable. I feel the same way about spiritual things and am usually disturbed by things that, though they sound right, seem unattainable. I am certainly not saying I lean on natural understanding, because I often make decisions only on faith when everything seems impossible. I do so *if* I believe whatever I am pursuing is attainable. This may sound contradictory, but it really is not, because if God guided me, it must be attainable.

When I first committed my life to Christ, I began experiencing a tangible relationship with Him. From the very beginning, because of my practical nature, I made a personal request to Him: "Lord, I just stepped away from a life of empty religion filled with hoops and loops that failed to reveal you or change me. I now know you are real and personal, but I need to see your direct relevance to my day-to-day life—at my job where I spend my waking hours and have my greatest challenges. I need to see you there!"

And God did just that. As the CEO and owner of the leading optical business in the Republic of Trinidad and Tobago at the time, God led me down a path of intense trials, faith, and revelation that launched me into becoming a well-known leader of the Faith at Work movement in the Caribbean. I had a deep passion to share my experiences and help people in the workplace understand their calling and authority to bring the Kingdom of God into day-to-day life and business. As I experienced God in so many relevant ways, I simply had to encourage others to believe in order to experience more.

My involvement led to hosting meetings and conferences both in Trinidad and abroad. At a local level, I was the president of the local chapter of the International Christian Chamber of Commerce and produced a radio program called *God at Work*. I shared biblical workplace principles and experiences that spoke to a wide spectrum of believers, from store clerks to bank executives.

My influence expanded beyond denominational walls and led to my hosting a national event in conjunction with the Global Day of Prayer in May 2005. Over eight thousand people, including bishops and leaders of all Christian denominations, came together to humble ourselves and pray in unity for our nation. Never before had all Christian denominations come together in genuine unity. It was a tremendously moving and successful experience. It was even positively reported by all of the local media and on the front pages of the three national newspapers.

In short, I was seeing results! I was poised to take this first step of unity to the next level. The various denominations looked for me to lead in the next step. It all meant a lot for me because I had desired for years to see the Church become more effective through putting aside differences and coming together as His Body. I wanted to see tangible evidence that things could really change in my country. As a neutral body, the Christian Chamber of Commerce had drawn everyone together in a way that one denomination could not do.

Everything I was working for was coming together after many years of hard work and sacrifice. Bear in mind that during all of this, I ran a company with 160 employees; I was a senior leader in my church; I produced radio broadcasts three times a week, and I was a father of seven children under the age of eleven at the time. The truth is, I was in a state of chronic stress. I slept very little and had dark circles around my eyes for a number of years. (Seriously, I looked like a raccoon.)

However, immediately after that unifying event, something unexpected happened. The best way I can describe it would be that someone shut off my power switch. I felt like God's grace had completely stopped flowing. Everything I was used to doing suddenly became extremely difficult to do. I felt like I was swimming in thick mud. To put it mildly, I became really confused.

GO AHEAD AND JUMP!

In an effort to solve the problem, I began making adjustments to my life. I took an extended rest, put all ministry on hold, and delegated most of the running of my company to others over the next six months. But still, nothing changed. By then, I was really baffled. There were time-sensitive decisions to make regarding this new unity effort. Confused, I started crying out to God for answers in January of 2006.

As I sat in my office praying one morning, a thought suddenly and clearly popped into my head, *Go talk to Johnny*. Johnny Enlow pastored a prophetic church in Atlanta at the time. I had met him earlier through some marketplace ministry events. I was in Trinidad at the time, so I shook off the thought. After half an hour, it came again—abnormally sudden, distinct, and clear: *Go talk to Johnny!* This time I paid attention!

I realized God was speaking to me. I booked a flight and was sitting with Johnny in his office in Atlanta the next afternoon.

God used that time together to open my eyes enough to see that He wanted me to get off the speeding train and stop everything I was doing. It meant resigning from leadership of the business chamber, resigning from the board and ministry of my church, discontinuing my radio program—everything! It meant completely shutting down everything I thought I was supposed to be doing, everything I had prayed for as it related to ministry. It was a 180-degree turn, but it felt right in my spirit.

Something specific happened that day with Johnny that I will never forget. After I informed him that I was coming to Atlanta, he had asked a couple of his prophetic intercessors to pray for me and seek the Lord for direction on my behalf. By the time I got there the following morning, one of them had sent him a response. This is what she said:

> I saw Colin on a pirate ship. He was walking the plank. He was not doing so because he had committed a crime or was being forced off the ship. He was doing so because he saw it as a way of escape from the crowd of people on the ship who were all pulling at him to get involved in their different organizations and ministries.
>
> Then the Lord showed up and told Colin, "Jump! Go ahead and jump off the ship! Because I'm about to do something very different going forward. It will not be through all of these organizations and people. It will just be you and Me."

I cannot tell you how relieved I felt at the time! For many years, I had been exposed to a lot of gifted prophetic people and had been given prophetic messages that spoke of seemingly never-ending training and stretching. So when the Lord showed up, I expected to hear, *Man up! Stay on the ship!* But instead, He said to jump, even if it meant into the vast ocean by myself. Although this message seemed opposed to all I had been working towards, my heart leapt with relief.

I made the decision to stop everything and will never forget the overwhelming peace I felt at the time. Then Johnny said something so profound it has become a phrase I often use to express my core message.

"Do you realize what she said?" Johnny asked. "She said the ship was a pirate ship! Pirates go after legitimate treasure in illegitimate ways!" He went on to stress that pirates do not chase after fool's gold and costume jewelry; they go after the real thing but in illegitimate ways.

I began to see how this described what has been happening to the Church to a significant extent. Countless ministries desire to see God's Kingdom built. They desire to see everyone come into a life-changing relationship with God. They desire to see miracles. They desire to see God move in their midst. All of these are genuine *treasures* to seek after, but so many of them are going about it in the illegitimate ways of natural man.

All of these are genuine treasures to seek after, but so many of them are going about it in the illegitimate ways of natural man.

They have overly-structured institutions with huge budgets and unnecessary assets that were never built at the direction of the Spirit of God. Many try to control and manipulate followers in order to build their own empires. As those empires get built, the focus becomes keeping the plates spinning rather than seeking the Spirit's direction for His Kingdom.

AN UNEXPECTED MOVE

One week after my trip to meet with Johnny, I was having a discussion with a friend who mentioned his desire to emigrate to Canada. In an instant, an overpowering chain reaction of thoughts consumed me. Right then and there, the idea was born to emigrate to a small town in Iowa, my wife's rural hometown.

Naturally, the idea seemed ridiculous. It was impractical, illogical, and not something I had considered before. Not only was I already walking away from all the ministry I had felt called to, but this move would mean walking away from everything else that defined my life. I would be leaving behind the day-to-day leadership of my business, friends, culture, and country.

Within a week, however, my wife and I were both sure the move was God's leading. We made the decision on a Sunday. The very next day, a construction company had been scheduled to start a major remodeling of an old house we had bought. I called the contractor who had worked with me for years building optical stores for my business and told him my predicament. He graciously understood, and the project was immediately canceled.

By the end of that week, we had found the house in Iowa we would eventually buy. It was a very large house, but it was offered at a good price. It was not even yet on the market, but we were able to view it fully online because it was a bed and breakfast inn at the time. By the end of the same week, someone also signed a contract to buy our house for exactly what we wanted with no realtor involved. By this time, our heads were spinning!

When we made the decision to move to Iowa, I had told my wife, who was three-and-a-half months pregnant with child number eight, that we needed to do this within four months because I was concerned about her not being able to fly during the later stage of pregnancy. But we were completely naive as to the realities of me as a Trinidadian obtaining permanent residency in just four months! It was only when we landed in the U.S. four months later and were greeted by the receiving immigration officer that we fully understood what God had done.

"Welcome to America, Mr. Ferreira!" he said. "It must have taken a long time."

"What do you mean?" I replied.

"I'm sure it must have taken you at least two to three years to finally get through the process!" I was taken by surprise.

"Actually, it was all done in under four months!" It was his turn to be surprised.

I could fill an entire chapter with the obvious miracles that got us through the process in that incredibly short time. Suffice it to say, God flung doors open repeatedly in ways only He could have done to get us to Iowa on time.

Often in hindsight, I understood why God wanted to do it through so many miracles. I was about to enter the most intense desert experience in my life. Only the miraculous testimonies of how we got there would give me the faith to believe I had not made a mistake and become shipwrecked amongst never-ending cornfields.

AN OPPORTUNITY TO ABORT

Moving to a new country was quite refreshing at first. Everything felt new—fresh experiences, a different culture, and a radically different climate. I began to rest and make up for lost time with my family after some intensely busy years. However, it didn't take too long for reality to begin to set in.

The first year and a half after I moved away, my company in Trinidad experienced a host of negative events. Flooding, an air conditioner unit exploding in a store, employee cars being stolen just weeks apart, a key employee being physically attacked by a homeless person on the city street—and the list went on. There were so many and seemingly so unrelated to each other that I began to sense they were part of some sort of attack by the enemy. I became very weary. After moving, I felt somewhat disconnected from the business and with the recent events, so I wanted to sell it and move on. I felt that after decades of managing the business through countless crises, I was ready to be done with it all.

A few months later, on a morning in early 2008, I got an unusual call from an American businessman who had been involved in establishing chains of successful optical businesses throughout the United States. He was interested in buying my business. After much prayer and consultation with some financial advisors, I agreed to engage in the process to sell.

Once we had established our confidentiality agreement, the audited financials were shared with him. His response after reviewing them was, "These financials are pristine!" In hindsight, that year was by far the peak of my company's performance to that date. We were in excellent financial condition and debt-free.

We agreed to meet in Trinidad for him to physically view the business, but during the visit, I began feeling a check in my spirit about selling. I felt the Lord saying that He had not yet fulfilled His plan and purpose for the business or the promises He had made. To sell it now would be like aborting a baby. There were a lot of specific things prophesied about the company that had not yet come to pass, but I was weary and tempted to cash in. On the other hand, I have always tried to seek after God's perfect will as opposed to His permissible will. I wanted to see exactly what He had in mind all along, not settle for what might be acceptable. As I mentioned earlier, when we refuse to settle is when we are most blessed, as His perfect will is allowed to be fulfilled.

During that visit with the potential buyer, I pulled the plug on proceeding any further with selling. I remember him saying, "But you don't even know what I am prepared to offer!" My response was that the amount was irrelevant because I did not feel I was supposed to sell.

We all know what had happened within a couple of months of that time—the global financial crisis of 2008.

A DOWNWARD TURN

Prior to that time, Trinidad and Tobago was the largest supplier of natural gas to the United States. We supplied over seventy-five percent of all of the natural gas imported by the United States. Hard to believe, but true! As a result, Trinidadians have often been called the Arabs of the Caribbean with a considerably stronger economy than most of the other Caribbean islands.

Then came fracking, a new technology developed in the United States to extract oil and gas from previously unreachable deposits. This turned the U.S. into a major producer overnight and cut imports from Trinidad. It also slashed the global prices of oil and gas. The economy there has been struggling ever since these developments in the oil and gas industries.

Adding to all of this, our Caribbean university, the University of the West Indies, opened a school of optometry for the Caribbean about six years ago. Unfortunately, almost all of the students are Trinidadian and want to work in Trinidad, creating an all-new crisis for my company. The number of optical stores on the island has doubled over the last ten years. With our poor economy and the doubling of competitors, the business situation had already become extremely difficult. Now that we have had to shut all of our stores due to COVID-19, the situation appears impossible.

Has it crossed my mind lately that I should have sold the business at that seemingly perfect time in 2008? Well, how I view this impossible mountain I seem to be up against at the time of this writing has everything to do with the central message of this book.

Chapter 3

THE DESERT OF MIDIAN

After moving to Iowa, the next thirteen years proved to be the most difficult desert experience of my life. When talking with close friends, I would even interchange the name *Iowa* with the name *Midian* in reference to what Moses probably experienced after leaving Egypt.

After having defended an Israelite slave being attacked by an Egyptian, Moses fled for his life into the wilderness and ended up in the rural desert community of Midian for forty years. His remarkable life story of divine intervention and the promises relating to his destiny seemed to have taken a wrong turn. No doubt it seemed all his training from living in Pharaoh's palace, the hub of worldly government at the time, had been for naught. I came to know a similar feeling amongst the Iowa cornfields.

After the 2008 financial crash and all the business challenges that followed, I also struggled personally. I was used to leading a lot of challenging projects and engaging with a lot of people on a daily basis. I'm a leader and pioneer by nature, who loves to start new things and lead them to achieve tangible results.

As the dust started settling from the move to Iowa, that awful feeling of being under house arrest began creeping in. Month after month, I seemed to be doing things that had to be done but which had little significant value in comparison to my former life. From my perspective, becoming more involved with my family was the only positive aspect of my new life. I engaged a bit with the kids' homeschooling, but that was more my wife's domain. I wasn't comfortable doing it, and candidly, I didn't particularly enjoy it. It did seem I was making up for a lot of lost time, as we had a lot of memorable family times together.

On the downside, however, my personal struggles and confusion about my purpose for being there caused me to be depressed and irritable at times. Personal character weaknesses that had been easily hidden from my family simply by not being with them all the time could no longer be hidden. I began to feel like a failure on a number of fronts. I started to sound like a broken record, repeatedly failing and asking my wife and kids for forgiveness.

The culture I encountered in Iowa also increased my sense of isolation. I came from a Caribbean culture with a lot of close and lasting friendships. I suppose the simple reality of living on an island meant you stayed reasonably close to friends no matter where you moved. In addition, the warm climate promoted an equally warm and connective culture.

My wife and I both love hospitality and would routinely open our home to others for meals, pool gatherings, grilling, outdoor movies in the summer, and Christmas parties in the winter. However, our hospitality generally seemed one-sided in Iowa. We often heard, "We really want to have you over soon!" But then, most of the time, nothing would come of it.

I had always been interested in experiencing the four seasons after spending forty-nine years living in a tropical climate. I had been exposed to many cold, snowy experiences through my travels and from living in Canada for one year when I was fifteen years old. However, the reality of really living in a cold climate as an adult was a rude awakening for this Trinidadian! I was not used to this thing called *winterizing*. I was not used to having to shut down a pool for nine months out of the year and watch intense winter storms destroy twelve different pool covers in thirteen years. I did not realize Iowa winters would be so long and dreary being surrounded by empty cornfields in every direction.

Then when spring came, everyone scurried around like wild mice trying to fit everything into a few warm months—every child's ball game, family camping and reunions, road trips, and house repairs to name a few. All of it made it quite challenging to truly connect with people. This new environment didn't seem to be a better quality of life. Now, the things I used to do all throughout a year were limited to a three- or four-month window.

I felt like a colorful, squawky parrot looking for a palm tree to land on—in Iowa. Good luck! Please understand, my intention is not to criticize Iowa. I simply was not wired for it, and what I encountered there added immensely to my desert experience.

UNLESS THE LORD BUILDS THE HOUSE

On top of all of it, one of the greatest thorns in my side while trying to understand and find purpose in Iowa proved to be our house. Yet it also turned out to be one of the most significant tools in the Lord's hand to do His deeper work in me and bring forth the message of this book.

Our 6,500 sq. ft. home had originally been a 1,500 sq. ft, 103-year-old little farmhouse. It was remodeled during the '70s and

'80s, and then a 5,000 sq. ft. addition was added to bring it to its present size. A banker with grand ideas had remodeled it and spent unusual amounts of money on such things as an indoor hot tub and sauna, a swimming pool sunken into a large deck, wrought iron and brick column fencing, eight bedrooms and bathrooms, and even a real fire pole inside the house. The house size was fantastic for my large family, particularly when we were pent up for months on end during winter.

However, as soon as we moved in, problems began to surface. The bulk of the remodeling had been done twenty-five to thirty-five years earlier, so almost everything began to expire at the same time. As fast I had one thing repaired, something else would go wrong. Within a couple of years, I had replaced all three heating and cooling systems, the entire roof, the pool liner, and quite a bit of the old wooden siding.

To be candid, I battled with God over this house because some years before I left Trinidad, people told me on two separate occasions that this would happen. They each came to me out of the blue and told me they felt God was going to give me a very large house that would need some work, and I wouldn't be able to refuse it because of the price I would get it for. When I bought the house in Iowa, it seemed like a deal, because housing is so expensive in Trinidad. I had been able to buy the large Iowa house for less than what I sold my 2,100 sq. ft. house in Trinidad. At the time I bought it, I knew it was the house God intended for us. But as time went on, it began to feel like a bottomless money pit.

To further add to my stack of challenges, during this time I had sought to invest a sizable part of my savings in different investments and lost most of it when the financial crash took place in 2008. I seemed to be losing money in every direction. My business in

Trinidad was struggling from the crash; I had lost a lot through those investments, and the house continued to absorb more money. Then I discovered that the roofing job I had done was a disaster. The entire roof needed to be redone again. The siding continued to leak and really needed to be completely replaced with a more suitable material. And on further inspection, thirty-two windows needed to be replaced.

Overwhelmed and frustrated, my life seemed stressful, senseless, purposeless, and heading for a crash. I wrestled with God: *Why? Why did you lead me to Iowa? Why this house? It makes no sense!*

Within moments, a clear and convicting thought popped into my mind as the Lord answered: *Do you have the money to fix the house?*

No! Then I sensed Him asking again. This time I answered, *No... not really! I lost a lot of my savings. I have nine kids that have to go to college and are all still in my house! Besides, you know that I'm not entitled to Social Security because I never worked in the U.S. How am I supposed to deal with all that is ahead?*

He asked again, *Do you have the money to fix the house?*

This time I bowed my head and answered honestly, *Yes, I do... but not much more.*

Then fix it properly, He answered. Then He continued, *There are many people living from paycheck to paycheck, trusting Me to provide month-by-month. I am not saying that it is what I want for everyone all of the time, but you want a back-up plan in case your business fails—the business you gave to me and I promised to watch over!*

You want to have a backup plan in case I fail you! Have I not provided everything you needed? Did I not say to be anxious for nothing? Did I not say, take no thought for tomorrow? Why should that not apply to you?

Son, I want you to know just who you are to Me! You are deeply concerned about your Fatherly responsibilities. Guess what! You got that trait from Me. Watch and rest in My care and My love for you. Fix the house.

I immediately hired a local contractor who came highly recommended. Over the course of a year, the house was beautifully transformed with a completely new roof, all new siding and trim, a new deck to replace the rotting one, and over thirty-two new windows. Not only did it look like a new house, but we corrected every fault discovered from the previous remodeling, and there were many of them. I have worked with many good contractors in my lifetime, but these people were like angels sent by God, easy to work with, and everything done right!

Around the same time I began to see the house situation more clearly, I came to the revelation that I did not understand how God *really* sees me. I hadn't fully realized how I am seen in heaven, or of my identity and the weight of it. I had not grasped during my decades of Christianity what perfect love my Father had for me—His beloved son. I felt God would withhold His blessing from me because of certain weaknesses in my life that didn't quite measure up to His standards. It felt like a subtle punishment—the overwhelming events, the move to a strange place,

What most of us do not realize is the extent to which the enemy has distorted God and the Gospel.

culture, and climate, the lack of a sense of purpose and value, the massive house issues, and my depleting finances. All happening while having ten others to care for!

All of it combined to feel as if I had taken a wrong turn in a maze and couldn't turn back. The only way out was for the Holy Spirit to open my eyes to the truth of how He sees me so that faith could arise to stand on this truth: "I know the thoughts I have towards you, says the Lord; thoughts of peace and not of evil, to give you a future and a hope." (Jeremiah 29:11 NKJV)

Over the next seven years, God began to open my eyes to things I had never seen before, even as a mature Christian leader. He revealed not only who He really is and who I am, but also the extent of deception within the religious system that has mixed traces of truth with carefully crafted lies to cripple God's people. What most of us do not realize is the extent to which the enemy has distorted God and the Gospel.

They say God works in mysterious ways, but that old adage put it too mildly when it came to that big old house. When I was first told by those two people that God was leading me to such a house, I had no idea the pain and distress it would cause. Yet His mysterious ways were evident because, in so many other ways, the house was an obvious blessing. My wife and I had a large master suite at one end of the house with a pretty cool office space in a corner and a turret-type enclosure. My two daughters were in another master suite at the other end of the house, and there were ample rooms and bathrooms for our seven boys.

Another way God mysteriously worked through that house began coming to light as the house was being transformed. During my personal morning time with the Lord one day, I asked Him about the house (as I so often did then). He began revealing spiritual parallels to the different house repairs being done. When He first led us to Iowa, His first focus had been to begin a new work on the head of our household—me. He needed to reveal some hidden things that hindered me from being the spiritual covering my family needed me to be. This work in me was paralleled by the roof of the physical house that needed to be properly restored.

As I mentioned earlier, the roof was actually done twice. The first time a contractor had convinced me to cover the old shingles with steel shingles. His reasoning was primarily to avoid stripping the old shingles, which we later discovered were as many as six layers deep in some places! Over time, we discovered those steel shingles were a bad choice for my roof which had countless angles and valleys.

There is a significant spiritual parallel here. In Romans 12:1, the Apostle Paul says we are to be transformed by the renewing of our minds. This transformation requires that old thinking be replaced with new thinking. If I do not remove the old and replace it with the new, I become double-minded and ineffective as the spiritual head of my family. There were new things God wanted to reveal to me, but it would require removing some existing beliefs.

Likewise, the replacing of worn-out leaking windows represented the work God was doing to seal off unwanted openings—some little and unseen, and others more obvious—that were having a negative spiritual impact on our family. The old window glass also had unusual etched patterns that hindered the view and looked very dated. I felt God was saying I was going to begin to see clearly from now on and not through the dated, religious ways.

Of course, replacing the siding naturally provided better insulation and protection from the harsh elements outside. But it also provided a completely new, long-lasting, and beautiful appearance, impenetrable to destructive elements. To make the parallel evident here, when our belief system is built with weak concepts, we have a weak spiritual immune system. It allows any destructive element or virus to penetrate and threaten life within. I believe God was building a new spiritual immune system for my family based on a much clearer understanding of our true identity. It wasn't simply an extreme makeover for the house, but a whole new makeover for our family's spiritual health and wholeness.

Last but not least of the spiritual parallels was the fence around the property. Houses in small towns in rural Iowa almost never had fences and walls around the entire property. But this one did. The elaborate fencing included hundreds of feet of brick walls and columns with wrought iron panels and gates between many segments. The entire west side of the property had all the brick columns in place but the fifteen-foot wide wrought iron panels between the columns were missing. They simply had never been completed. On the south side, the columns and wrought iron were all there but in serious need of repair. For decades, this expensive fence had been neglected and never finished.

As much as I was fed up with pouring money into the house, something within me compelled me to get it *all* done. In many ways, I felt as if the fence represented something similar to the Jews needing to rebuild the wall around Jerusalem in the days of Nehemiah. Doing so was a critical part of Jerusalem being restored to its intended glory. They could no longer be easily plundered by enemies. This analogy also represented what God was doing with me and my family as He rebuilt our walls with new revelation and truth. No longer would we be so vulnerable to attacks of accusations and fear from our spiritual enemies. We were all learning to stand strong, secure, and confident as children of a loving and almighty Father at a level beyond our previous understanding.

After repairs to the entire fence wall were completed in 2017, I commissioned two of my sons to paint 150 feet of wrought iron in the summer of 2018. When they were done, I walked around the house and the yard. Quite unexpectedly, an unusual peace came over me with the thought that I was completely done! That word *done* seemed to have a finality to it. At the time, I had no idea that just a few months later during a prayer meeting with friends, God would tell us our time was up in Iowa. My thirteen years of desert experience was coming to an end.

THE DAM BROKE!

When we first felt the leading of God telling us it was time to move again, there was such a sense of excitement and release that there was no doubt God was directing us. We had absolutely no idea where we were to move, so we asked Him. In two days, He basically pointed us to Georgia. I can't easily explain why. We have no family in Georgia nor anything else happening there. There was just a confident sense and peace that Georgia was it. (Incidentally, it turned out that my publisher lives almost next door to me.)

During the many years of my desert struggle, I knew not to take matters into my own hands and attempt to leave Iowa without God's release to do so. I always had the strong sense that I was the person who would end up in the belly of a whale like Jonah did if I attempted to walk away from what God was doing with me. He had invested too much into me to let me walk away. Besides, I felt certain that if I ever attempted to do so, I simply would not be able to leave Iowa because it would take a miracle to sell a 6,500 sq ft home in a little rural town where the average home size was around 2,500 sq ft. And it would take yet another miracle to recover all the money poured into it over the years.

But then I texted a friend about our decision to move. His response completely blew us away! He had sold his own business to a young successful businessman from the area who had just asked him six weeks earlier if he thought I would consider selling my house. It seemed too good to be true, especially after the last difficult decade. He came to see the house, and in three days we settled on a price I thought was right but never hoped to get. There was no realtor involved, plus he offered to buy without any inspections or contingencies! God was moving fast and in a jaw-dropping way. And it could never have happened if I had not fixed the house properly.

God still had one final and encouraging lesson to teach me from that house. As we were preparing to move, I sat one morning in my usual place where I spent time with God. As I did so, something came to mind very strongly. Out in the far corner of my backyard was an odd, rectangular fenced-in area, about eight feet square, that had been placed there by the previous owners. The six-foot-tall decrepit wooden fence kept me from seeing what was inside. As I stretched to look over, I saw what looked like an old rusty wagon and other unrecognizable metal junk. There was also a wild, fifteen-foot-tall mulberry tree growing in the middle. Because our yard was large and the junk wasn't visible, I had put off dealing with it for the thirteen years we had lived there. That morning, however, I had a strong conviction that I should clean it up and not leave it there for the new owner.

So, that afternoon, I headed to the backyard and proceeded to dismantle the fence. Once it was down, I discovered the rusty wagon I had originally seen and, to my surprise, a rusty old sleigh, as well. When I tried to remove it, I discovered the mulberry tree's roots had grown around the base of the sleigh making it impossible to move. A friend and I worked for some time with an assortment of saws to release the sleigh from the root of the tree. When it was done, I stood looking at that strange sleigh sitting in my yard just wondering at the oddness of it. I suppose because God had been speaking to me so often, I asked Him, *Father, what is this about? I feel like you want to tell me something!*

Right then, I felt Him saying to me, *Son, you are now free to glide effortlessly in a way you have never done before! There were deeply rooted false teachings and doctrines that had held you back and continue to hold back many of My people.*

From the journey I was on, it was clear to me He was referring to the network of deeply established religious lies he had been exposing that make it difficult for us to move, much less glide into our future with grace, peace, and joy. These are lies about God, His nature, how He sees us and really feels toward us. They are lies about our new nature, our sonship, our true righteousness, and much more. These lies and distortions of doctrine keep us from ever reaching the full potential God planned for our lives.

I believe the releasing of that sleigh was a prophetic act, symbolic of what had taken place in Iowa, my Midian desert. My encounter with that sleigh was my burning bush experience revealing my present mission.

In the rest of this book, I'll unravel a lot of these lies and false doctrines and open up some of the mysteries of God. I will begin with those relating to God, His heart, and His identity. Thereafter, I will shed light on where the Church is today, who we *really* are to God, and talk about our new nature in ways many have never heard before.

My prayer is that it will be the beginning of a transformation of your mind that will surely bring a big smile to your face and joy to your heart.

WHO IS GOD...REALLY?

Chapter 4

A GOD WHO HIDES HIMSELF

"Truly...you are a God who hides Himself."
—ISAIAH 45:15 TPT

Throughout this book, much of what I'll be sharing are actually mysteries of God. That should come as no surprise. We all know that Jesus often spoke in parables and, on some occasions, would explain the true meaning of the parables only to His chosen disciples:

And with many such parables He spoke the word to them as they were able to hear it. But without a parable He did not speak to them. And when they were alone, He explained all things to His disciples. (Mark 4:33-34 NKJV)

As we've read those parables, no doubt we subconsciously thought the concealing was for the undiscerning Israelites of that time and not us. We have been led to believe that, generally, Christians have been taught to understand these mysteries. But why should we think we understand all of the key mysteries that we need to know when the evidence is undeniable that the Church is not where it is supposed to be? Clearly, we are falling so short. Perhaps we don't understand all we think we do.

Now you may think, *I don't expect to understand all things about God, so what's the big deal if there are some mysteries I never understand?* The problem is this: when you do not believe something the way it is supposed to be, you simply will believe something else. When it comes to God's truth, replacing it with something else always has detrimental consequences. These consequences may not lead to sin, but they may, at the least, keep us from experiencing the fullness of God's perfect plan and destiny for our lives. It keeps us weak and anemic spiritually. Unfortunately, many people seem to be content with that. Not me! I'm always fighting to understand: *If God said it, why can't I experience it?*

One factor contributing to why so many people settle for less is that they are easily influenced by numbers. If a lot of Christians believe something, they think, it must be right or at least acceptable. We are even quicker to endorse such views if we might face hard challenges for choosing the other direction.

As a result, too many Christians happily settle for what I call God's permissible will as opposed to His perfect will. For example, when I accepted Christ at the age of twenty-seven, I had come out of a life of constant dating as a single man. Shortly after my conversion, I felt led to ask God to choose my wife for me, because I did not trust my own judgment. I knew my criteria in the past were superficial and could get me into trouble. I told God I did not have a clue what He had planned for my life in twenty or thirty years and no idea what kind of person I would need then. I decided I would completely stop dating until I felt Him bring someone into my life.

I waited seven long, lonely years, not dating until He eventually sent my future wife from Iowa to Trinidad on a mission trip. Seven months later, we were married. Now, twenty-nine years later, I cannot imagine life without her or our nine kids. (By the way, we both said we wanted one, maybe two children. God had other plans.)

Would I have done something wrong to marry someone else? Certainly not, but I would not be where I am today without her. I am certain of that. I'm so thankful for our wonderful, intimate relationship and the faith we share during these tumultuous times we are presently in. So is it really okay not to understand the fullness of what God wants for us and simply settle for what He permits?

TREASURES OF DARKNESS

As I was living out what felt like a dark and isolated experience in Iowa, God used that time to reveal mysteries I thought I already understood, but in reality, did not—even as a church and ministry leader for many years. As God says in Isaiah, "I will give you the treasures of darkness and hidden riches of secret places...." (Isaiah 45:3 NKJV)

In a previous chapter, I shared that a key focus of this book is to more deeply reveal God's primary purpose for sending Jesus—to give us a new identity as His children and reveal Himself to us. I believe that this is the proper platform from which a powerful and effective Church will be revealed in these times. The real depth of this truth is still a mystery to most believers. However, if this primary purpose is significant to God, to not grasp it in its fullness would be detrimental, perhaps even dangerous, for His Church.

I am convinced that the season we are now moving into has a lot to do with a global move of God through disruption of church as usual for the revealing of the sons and daughters of God, as Paul describes in his letter to the Romans: "For the creation waits in eager expectation for the children of God to be revealed." (Romans 8:19 NIV)

What really baffled me was that there were things I had read over and over, but only in that period of dark distress in Iowa did they begin to be revealed differently. As this fresh perspective became clearer, I became increasingly concerned that I might be drifting away from what the vast majority of Christian believers had accepted as *the* full truth.

As time passed, however, more Scripture was revealed that supported this deeper understanding of God's primary purpose and its implications for us. The more I saw and understood, the more it became too overwhelming to ignore or refute. Scripture passages like these encouraged me to keep digging into the mysteries of God:

Then He said to them, "Be diligent to understand the meaning behind everything you hear, for *as you do, more understanding will be given to you.* And according to the depth of your longing to understand, much more will be added to you. For *those who listen with open hearts will receive more revelation.* But those who don't listen with open hearts will lose what little they think they have." (Mark 4:24-25 TPT, *emphasis added*)

This is why the Scriptures say: *Things never discovered or heard of before*, things beyond our ability to imagine—these are the many things God has in store for all His lovers. But God now unveils these profound realities to us by His Spirit. Yes, *He has revealed to us His inmost heart and deepest mysteries through the Holy Spirit* who constantly explores all things. After all, who can really see into a person's heart and know his hidden impulses except for that person's spirit? So it is with God. His thoughts and secrets are only fully understood by His Spirit, the Spirit of God. (1 Corinthians 2:9-11 TPT, *emphasis added*)

A great deal of what I will be exposing in the pages to follow has been cloaked by God Himself. To cloak means to hide, cover, or disguise. For example, one might say a mission was cloaked in mystery. I am completely convinced that God passionately loves mankind and desires for all of us to come to a full knowledge of Him. However, because of His wisdom and understanding of the hearts of men, God has chosen to cloak this revelation from those who are determined to maintain a religious mind and the letter of the law—even within the new covenant. I'll explain more of what that means as we move forward, but most of what is ahead in this book will challenge you to search out the heart of God and find what He has chosen to hide from the wisdom of man.

The good news is that He has already promised to do just that: "And you will seek Me and *find* Me, *when* you *search* for Me with *all* of your *heart*." (Jeremiah 29:13 NKJV, *emphasis added*) This is certainly not about following the crowd. It's not about the quantity of searching or the intellectual level of the searcher as much as it is about the quality (motive) of the heart.

Let me share a few more Scriptures that reveal how intentional God has been in keeping His truth cloaked:

Whenever Jesus addressed the crowds, He always spoke in allegories. He never spoke without using parables. (Matthew 13:34 TPT)

Then Jesus added, shouting out to all who would hear, "Listen with your hearts and you will understand. (Luke 8:8b TPT)

And consider this lengthier passage from Matthew's account of the words of Jesus:

Then His disciples approached Jesus and asked, "Why do you always speak to people in these hard-to-understand parables?"

He explained, "You've been given the intimate experience of insight into the hidden truths and mysteries of the realm of heaven's Kingdom, but they have not. For everyone who listens with an open heart will receive progressively more revelation until he has more than enough. But those who don't listen with an open, teachable heart, even the understanding that they think they have will be taken from them. That's why I teach the people using parables, because they think they're looking for truth, yet because their hearts are unteachable, they never discover it. Although they will listen to Me, they never fully perceive the message I speak. The prophecy of Isaiah describes them perfectly:

Although they listen carefully to everything I speak,
they don't understand a thing I say.
They look and pretend to see,
but the eyes of their hearts are closed.
Their minds are dull and slow to perceive,
their ears are plugged and are hard of hearing,
and they have deliberately shut their eyes to the truth.
Otherwise, they would open their eyes to see,
and open their ears to hear,
and open their minds to understand.
Then they would turn to Me
and let Me instantly heal them.

But your eyes are privileged, for they see. Delighted are your ears, for they are open to hear all these things. Many prophets and godly people in times past yearned to see these days of miracles that you've been favored to see. They would have given everything to hear the revelation you've been favored to hear. Yet they didn't get to see as much as a glimpse or hear even a whisper. (Matthew 13:10-17 TPT)

GOD'S FAMILY

I spoke at a Seven Mountains conference hosted by Marketplace Leaders in Atlanta in 2008 on the Mountain of Family. During a plenary session and afternoon workshop, I focused on Malachi 4:5-6: "Behold, I will send you Elijah the prophet before the coming of the great and dreadful day of the Lord. And he will turn the hearts of the fathers to the children and the hearts of the children to their fathers, lest I come and strike the earth with a curse." (NKJV)

My wife and I had a scheduled meeting with a prophet for prayer and prophetic ministry right after my session. A couple of years before then, he had prayed with me very briefly, but I had not known him otherwise nor had any connection with him. After my workshop and spending a few moments speaking with workshop participants, we eagerly rushed to the elevators to make it to our appointment with him. We briefly introduced ourselves, and the prophet began to pray. What follows is a small part of the transcript. Because of the topic I had been teaching just moments ago, the beginning got my immediate attention:

I saw this word written on a sword just now. It says Malachi 4: 5 and 6, "Behold, I will send you Elijah the prophet before the coming of the great and dreadful day of the Lord. And He will turn the hearts of the fathers to the children, and the hearts of the children to their fathers, lest I come and strike the earth with a curse." (NKJV) The Lord showed me a sword; it came out of heaven. It was a golden sword, and on the sword is written that Scripture. And from this day forth you will move into a new place. God says, "I'm going to use you as one that's going to manifest that Scripture." I see the words *family values* are going to be something that is going to come forth in your ministry in this next season. The Lord says you're coming out of the business mountain and realm. "I'm moving you into a new realm, even into the family realm," says the Lord.

God says, "I've called you as one who's going to begin to release the father anointing and cause men to come to be fathers and to be men under the authority of God. I'm going to cause you to be a man of great wisdom that is able to cause these men to rise up. There's going to be an anointing on you to break them out of pornography; there's going to be an anointing on you to break them out of alcoholism; there's going to be an anointing on you to break them out of drug addiction. You're going to see that there's a fresh deliverance anointing that will come upon you, and it's going to cause demons to flee. The way this anointing will work is going to be through the Father's embrace."

It took me some years to understand that those statements were a cloaked message that God would reveal in time. For some years after hearing them, I wondered how God would move me to focus on family ministry. I had done a lot of family-focused ministry in years past and regularly facilitated parenting classes, but that was primarily to find answers for my own growing family. I felt no passion to make it a focused ministry beyond understanding my personal family and helping others as I had the opportunity to do so. Something did not add up. In my experience, I could tell when God's grace points me in a particular direction, and, so far, He had not given me a heart for helping families as an intentional ministry to develop.

But I have learned over the years what the Scriptures say about prophecy: "For we know in part and prophesy in part." (1 Corinthians 13:9 NKJV) Often prophets themselves may not see the hidden message but only feel compelled to say what they sense the Lord wants them to say. Over the last decade, God has made that prophetic word abundantly clear to me, and it was not what I first thought. Permit me to share what He has shown me.

You may recall in the first chapter, I shared my name and its meaning. I explained that I believe its meaning (child) was significant in relation to my destiny and how I feel a strong calling to help transition God's people from being primarily servants to becoming confident children of God who better understand how to love Him and be loved.

In recent years, as I reread that prophetic word in light of the revelatory journey I have been on, I am blown away at what God has confirmed in my heart. The family ministry alluded to was really pertaining to our true spiritual Family. His mention of "family values" relates to Jesus' primary mission to give us the right to become God's actual children.

A MYSTERY REVEALED

A typical example of a significant but cloaked message from God is one that launches us into the meat of this book. The passage I mentioned earlier, Malachi 4: 5-6 had always baffled me. Why did God make this passage the very last thing He spoke through the prophets of old to mankind before going completely silent for hundreds of years?

> Behold, I will send you Elijah the prophet before the coming of the great and dreadful day of the Lord. And he will turn the hearts of the fathers to their children, and the hearts of the children to their fathers, lest I come and strike the earth with a curse. (Mal. 4:5-6 NKJV)

If someone is seriously interested in one's well-being and has a role that requires providing critical direction for their lives, we would expect the very last thing they say to be extremely important. Yet for many years, I could not understand how personal relationships between earthly fathers and children would place the entire world at risk of being cursed. Was that really the last thing God wanted to say to mankind before His period of silence?

Now, I am not saying relationships between fathers and their children are not important. Psychologists will attest to the many major problems we face in society as a result of poor father/child relationships. However, in the pages to come, you will see clearly that God's primary focus was to reconcile us as children into an intimate relationship with Him as our Abba, Father—far beyond our present realization. Thus, this was an intentionally cloaked message the Father is now fully revealing. His message was about how He would turn the hearts of His children to Himself as *the* Father.

The bottom line is that this book is about revealing mysteries of God. It's about hidden things God intended to disguise from those whose hearts are not willing to truly seek them out with pure motives. But to reveal those mysteries, we must unravel a complex system of religious lies that come from the very pit of hell. These lies accuse both

God and us to thwart God's ultimate plan for us. In short, we need not only to understand our place as sons and daughters of God our Father, but also to see how critical spiritual foundations have been twisted through religious misconceptions and the enemy's distortions.

So, whether you are a seminary-trained theologian or have recently become a Christian, I urge you to pray right now that God will guide you and reveal any truth you may be missing.

Chapter 5

WHO GOD IS AND IS NOT

When listening to many Christians pray over the years, I have noticed some revealing habits. For example, many people begin with "Heavenly Father" or "Dear Lord Jesus" and then, throughout the prayer, randomly switch back and forth between the two for no apparent reason. Occasionally, "Holy Spirit" also gets thrown into the mix.

It's as if we fire a shotgun loaded with scattershot up to heaven with the hope of connecting with someone, any one of the members of the Trinity. The end result is a lot of prayers that sound like we're pleading, I hope somebody can hear me! Anyone there?!

This scattered prayer habit betrays our lack of understanding of the three unique persons and roles within the Godhead. Our misunderstanding produces a lack of confidence when praying and hurts us in the courts of heaven where we are being accused.

For centuries, the Church has taught a mixed message of grace and law as Satan perpetually works to deceive us with a blend of truth and lies. Every denomination likes to believe that they have all the truth even if they say otherwise, but this kind of thinking does not give us eyes to see and ears to hear deeper revelation. Instead, we become stagnant and susceptible to deception.

The first thing I want to address is the issue of Satan being the accuser, but not in the limited way we usually think. Yes, we rightfully refer to Satan as the accuser of God's people. However, we usually fail to recognize his first goal—at which he has been extremely successful—is to accuse God to men. Actually, I am not sure who he accuses more, God or us. We see the first example of his accusing God in Genesis 3:1 when he suggested to Eve, "Has God indeed said...?"(NKJV)

Satan combines truth with lies to keep us from discovering how incredibly loving and engaging God really is.

Revelation 12:10 reveals that Satan accuses us day and night! He does it incessantly to cripple us with his number-one weapon—fear. Fear of not pleasing God, not measuring up to His expectations, not deserving His blessing and favor, having to fend for yourself and control your circumstances—the list is endless. But his accusations can have little effect if we truly understand God as He is and not as Satan accuses Him to be. Do not treat that statement lightly! Satan combines truth with lies to keep us from discovering how incredibly loving and engaging God really is. When we truly know Him, we begin to more fully understand how God really sees us. It is this understanding that brings us into true, lasting rest. To keep us from finding this rest, the enemy constantly seeks to twist our understanding of God.

Yet Jesus said as He was praying to the Father, "[T]his is *the way* to have eternal life—to *know* you, the one true God, and Jesus Christ, the one you sent to earth." (John 17:3 NLT, *emphasis added*) You may think you know where I am going with this, but I urge you to avoid assuming you already understand the depth of it. I have been a very active Christian for thirty-five years, leading and speaking in ministry for many of those years, and yet I am in awe of what God has been more deeply revealing to me about this over the last seven years. It has felt like I'm finally receiving the fullness of the Good News, and it is far better than most believers realize.

The following three Scriptures further confirm that really knowing God (as He truly is) is all that we really need to experience real-life (*emphasis added*):

> May God give you more and more *grace and peace as you grow in your knowledge of God and Jesus Christ our Lord.* (3) By *His* divine power, God has given us everything we need for living a godly life. *We have received all of this by coming to know Him,* the one who called us to Himself by means of His marvelous glory and excellence. (2 Peter 1:2-3 NLT)

> We ask God to give you *complete knowledge* of His will and to give you spiritual wisdom and understanding. (10) Then the way you live will always honor and please the Lord, and your lives will produce every kind of good fruit. *All the while, you will grow as you learn to know God better and better.* (Colossians 1:9b-10 NLT)

> This is what the Lord says: "Don't let the wise man boast in his wisdom, or the powerful boast in their power, or the rich boast in their riches. But those who wish to boast should boast in this alone: That they *truly know Me* and understand that I am the Lord who demonstrates unfailing love and who brings justice and righteousness to the earth, and I delight in these things. I, the Lord, have spoken!" (Jeremiah 9:23-24 NLT)

I have read these verses countless times, but it has only been in recent years that my eyes have opened to what was there all along. To truly know God as He is, not as Satan paints Him through religion, is to enter a far deeper and more active relationship with Him in the eternal realm with access to heaven's power and authority. The better we understand that all we are required to do is trust Him and accept His love, the more grace we receive, which is Christ working in and through us. We will experience true peace as we learn to enter His full rest as a child does. Thus Satan works incessantly to deceive us about these truths.

Here are just a few examples of subtle lies and accusations Satan makes against God:

- God is always sin-conscious because of His holiness.

- God calls you His son/daughter, but He will never see you quite like Jesus.

- God wants you to be like Jesus, His only true Son, holy and perfect, so work on it!

- God loves you, but He doesn't always like you.

- God is primarily focused on building character.

- God more often than not will find a reason why He should withhold blessing from you.

- God sent Jesus to be actively involved with you because it is beneath Him as God Almighty.

If we believe these lies and accusations against God, we are more apt to be deceived by Satan's accusations against us because they fit more with his distorted version of God. Look closely at each of the accusations above. They each appear to have some measure of truth in them but are actually twisted lies.

I'll clarify these deceptions as we go, but to illustrate the deception behind just the first point above, consider this: Yes, God is holy, but if Jesus paid for our sin to be *removed* from us as far as the east is from the west, why would God be sin-focused? This thinking makes *us* sin-focused, which causes us to drift from grace and step into condemnation and self-effort, not able to overcome sin. Sin is *not* acceptable, but the means to overcome it is not self-effort.

GLOBAL ENEMY NUMBER ONE

My wife and I went on our first cruise in 2017. I have always avoided cruises because of a propensity for sea-sickness, but this was a river cruise up the calm Rhine River that runs between Germany and France. We stopped along the river at various quaint towns and larger cities, but two stops in the cities of Strasburg and Cologne etched indelible memories for me.

These two cities are famous for massive cathedrals built many centuries ago. At one time, these were the tallest structures in the world at over 500 feet. To stand in front of these structures was a mind-boggling experience! It was hard to wrap my mind around the structural and intricate work involving approximately 600 years of countless man-hours and phenomenal amounts of money.

It is not my desire to offend anyone, but as I viewed these structures, a dark and disturbing feeling came over me. I could not understand how such structures could represent the relational God that I know. I felt Him saying to me regarding each cathedral, *This has nothing to do with Me! This is like a Tower of Babel! It is a complete misrepresentation of who I am and My truth.* I felt He was saying those structures were intended to make a powerful statement of religious and political power, dominance, intimidation, and control over the people. Who would dare to question the system that could produce such finances and imposing edifices in those days? Yet each structure seemed so gothic and dark with demonic gargoyles perched at every corner. Architectural and historical experts actually disagree on the purpose of these gargoyles. Some say it was to ward off evil spirits, while others insist it was to scare people into going to church and remind them of damnation apart from God.

Either way, these buildings did not reflect God as one who reaches out to man like the father in the prodigal story, but as one you cannot easily relate with and must cower before. Our tour guide explained there was a building nearby where convicted criminals were taken to be tortured in sadistic ways to force them to repent in an effort to save their souls before execution. Who would inspire such actions? Certainly not our Father. Needless to say, the depth of this revelation disturbed me for weeks afterward.

I was not dealing with little "white lies" but rather a massive deceptive system developed over centuries by a dark principality to keep man from knowing God as He really is.

Seeing these cathedrals made it clear I was not dealing with little "white lies" but rather a massive deceptive system developed over centuries by a dark principality to keep man from knowing God as He really is. I do not believe my encounter with those cathedrals was by chance because throughout this journey to better understand God, I have been coming to understand just how powerful the principality of religion is. If we are to see God for who He really is, we must be willing to dismantle and remove religious lies and structures.

Regardless of denominational affiliation, the modern times we live in, or what you say you believe, the influence of this system of religion has been embedded into our psyche for many generations.

A lot of what we believe and do as Christians today is rooted in this religious history.

At times, you may notice my using the word *religion* in a negative context. I am not referring to the strict dictionary definition of religion, as a particular system of faith and worship. By *religion*, I refer to *man's way of representing God*. These man-made systems of worshiping God involve rules, regulations, requirements, and acts of piety that are often not consistent with Scripture and do not reflect His true character or person.

I do not believe there is a more sinister, evil, or demonic principality on earth than this spirit of religion. This spirit has had a tremendous influence on the entire world for millennia. You may feel I have ventured too far by saying there is such a spirit, but hear me out. We do know Satan is the father of lies and accusations. His primary goal is to deceive us from ever coming into the authority, freedom, and joy God intended. Because of his hatred for God and His children, he works perpetually through accusations and deception to separate us from God and all that is rightfully ours.

Satan knows that in the absence of intimacy and true relationship, we tend to create our own perceptions of God.

Satan knows that in the absence of intimacy and true relationship, we tend to create our own perceptions of God. We develop our own understanding of how He should be approached, and Satan is more than willing and able to help us do so. As a result, we have so many different religions believing different things. It seems easy to look down on others who practice a different religion while our own understanding of a relationship with our Father may be far more skewed than we realize.

Once, as I drove with a friend to a meeting, he said to me, "I really want to become more intimate with God, but I don't know how to go beyond where I am! Do you have any ideas?" He talked about some obvious ways like spending quality time with God, prayer, worship, reading, and meditating on the Word.

Then there was a moment of quiet during which I felt the Lord impress something upon my heart to say. I told my friend that all of those things would certainly help, and are even necessary, but what if your core understanding of God is skewed to begin with? What if you believe God is love, but you have an underlying subconscious sense that He doesn't really like you? After all, we human beings can technically love someone but not really like to be around them too much. We may genuinely care about them but don't want to deal with their issues. And those people whom we might love but not like, probably wouldn't be too excited about hanging around with us anyway when they perceive how we feel about them.

The truth is we all have issues. If we believe God primarily focuses on those issues, how could we ever desire to become more intimate with Him? Aren't we drawn to those who accept us as we are? Do we not enjoy being around such people as opposed to those we think look down on us? Yet it is this condescending God that religion projects. To become more intimate with God, we have to actually want to be with Him. We do not feel that desire to be with Him because of a lot of false assumptions and wrong beliefs about Him. When we simply accept His acceptance and love, we have that intimacy. He then works by His grace and power to fix our issues and we naturally bear fruit (I will explain this in-depth in Chapter 11).

Once we begin to truly know God, we can't help but love Him more!

Removing false assumptions and coming to really know our Father requires us first to allow Him to reprogram our minds to see Him as He really is. Once we begin to truly *know* God, we can't help but love Him more! As 1 John 4:8 says, "He who does not love God, does not know God."(NKJV) Those who reject God only do so because they do not know Him as He is or have not heard of the true Him.

AN ACCURATE DESCRIPTION OF GOD

So, who is God? There are volumes written on this topic and no end to the answers or questions. For the purposes of this book, I am speaking more narrowly to the specific nature of the Father and the significance of the relationship intended between Himself and man. The best way I could think to begin is with a description from someone who knows Him better than anyone else—Jesus.

You may recall I referenced Luke 15 earlier, which contains the three parables usually titled *The Lost Sheep, The Lost Coin, and The Lost Son*. There is a common thread between the three parables. In each of them, someone lost something considered very precious. This loss was of such deep concern that the person primarily focused on recovering their precious possession. When it was eventually recovered, the owner experienced great joy and celebrated accordingly. This searching person Jesus is alluding to is none other than God Himself.

When I earlier mentioned the last parable of the prodigal, I focused on the religious leaders and the elder son. Now, let's turn our attention to the father.

What really struck me about him is this: Parables are known for fictional characters created to express an allegory. However, here Jesus is actually describing God the Father Himself! Jesus would not embellish the story and drift from the truth He wants to convey about the Father, so the father in the parable has to have the exact same desires, traits, and personality as God the Father. So, we are actually getting an accurate description of our heavenly Father directly from Jesus!

Let's look then at the parable from Luke 15:20-24 to see what he reveals about the Father:

And he arose and came to his father. But when he was still a great way off, his father saw him and had compassion, and ran and fell on his neck and kissed him. And the son said to him, "Father, I have sinned against heaven and in your sight, and am no longer worthy to be called your son." But the father said to his servants, "Bring out the best robe and put it on him, and put a ring on his hand and sandals on his feet. And bring the fatted calf and kill it and let us eat and be merry; for this my son was dead and is alive again; he was lost and is found." And they began to be merry. (NKJV)

The father sees the son from afar and literally *runs* to greet him with a kiss and hug. Do not miss this next point: The father doesn't even allow his son to finish his planned speech but instantly restores him to complete sonship. Doesn't this seem contrary to how most Christians view our heavenly Father?

If we were to rewrite the parable based on our perception of the Father, it would probably look more like this:

And he arose and came to his father. But when he was still a way off, his father saw him, had compassion for him but waited for him to come to the door. As the father stood silent at the door, the son said to him, "Father, I have sinned against heaven and before you and I am no longer worthy to be called your son, make me like one of your hired servants." After allowing the son to complete his entire repentance speech, the father answered, "I am happy to see you son. I am glad that you came to your senses. You really hurt me, but I forgive you. You are welcome back; come on in. However, we do need to work on some issues. You are a pretty messed up kid! You need to be more like your older brother...."

We humans do not easily understand what Jesus did for us at the cross, because our thinking is often quite different than the ways of heaven. By Jesus' death, all of our sin and all that made us morally unacceptable was permanently removed, so there is now no reason for the Father not to be completely delighted in us. Put simply: God is not sin-conscious! His focus is not on our sin. As a matter of fact, because of what Jesus did, all of our sin is so far removed from us, it's simply not there.

Does this mean that God could care less when we sin? Certainly not! As Paul said, we should not sin that more grace would abound (Romans 6:1-2) Does this mean that God does not discipline us? Certainly, He does! His fatherly love for us compels Him to do so for our own good. He desires that we have abundant life and not fall into the enemy's traps which are there to kill, steal, and destroy. The writer of Hebrews says the same: "But if you are without chastening, of which all have become partakers, then you are illegitimate and not sons." (Hebrews 12:8 NKJV)

The point is, we are new creations in whom God takes great delight. The more we understand this reality, the less condemnation we feel, and the better we can understand the full acceptance of the son by the father in the parable. (I know you may have some *but what about?* thoughts. Not to worry, we'll revisit those in Chapter 9.)

THE GODHEAD

At the beginning of this chapter, I talked about how most believers pray randomly to all three Persons of the Godhead. This scattered prayer approach shows a lack of understanding that the Godhead comprises three individual Persons. They are in unity and harmony as One, but they are also three separate Persons with distinctly different roles. Any attempt to visualize this mystery of the Trinity could never fully convey the reality, but consider this diagram I have found best explains the Godhead:

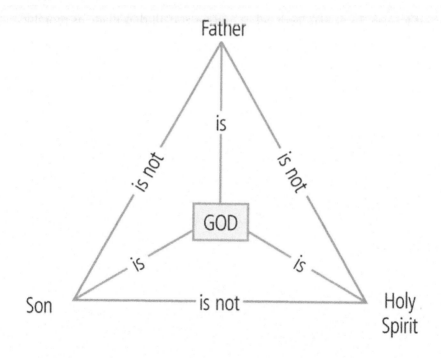

As the diagram demonstrates, while all three Persons comprise the Godhead, one is not the other. The Father is not Jesus nor vice versa. Neither is the Holy Spirit Jesus, and so on. Throughout the Scriptures, this truth is made clear as Jesus prays to the Father (e.g. John 17) and talks about how the Spirit only speaks what He hears from the Father and the Son. (John 16:12-13) These are just two of many examples.

Throughout the Gospels, we clearly see Jesus distinguishing between the three Persons of the Godhead. We see the Father sending Jesus to clear the way for our adoptions and the expansion of His family. We see Jesus constantly praying to the Father and directing us to a relationship with the Father just like He has. We know the Holy Spirit was sent by Him to be our comforter, counselor, teacher, etc. It is the Holy Spirit who dwells in us. I do not profess to perfectly understand the mystery of the Godhead, but there are distinctions between the three, and God has chosen to reveal this for our benefit.

Why is this reality so important? Why should I not pray randomly using the name of any of the three I choose? Aren't they all God? Well, it's not about rules—what you can and cannot do. What's important to truly grasp is that the Godhead is made up of three individual persons. There are relationships between the three. Because these relationships exist, the Father sent the Son to reconcile us to Himself (the Father) and for Jesus to also demonstrate how we can live in the same Father/son or Father/daughter relationship He and the Father enjoy. The Holy Spirit empowered the man Jesus while on earth and empowers us in the same way. It is

Failing to intentionally and predominantly live in the Father/child relationship God intended for us causes a servant mentality.

also important to understand that the type of relationship between the three persons of the Godhead has always existed as Father, Son, and Holy Spirit. We were created in His likeness to enjoy the same type of relationships.

Failing to intentionally and predominantly live in the Father/child relationship God intended for us causes a servant mentality. This mentality drifts in and out of faith and confidence because it relies on performance to relieve our subtle sense of failure and condemnation. All man-created religions differ from true Christianity in that they either demand servitude and performance or point to a non-relational God or force. On the other hand, true faith and rest comes from understanding and embracing Christianity's Father/child relationship.

Jesus knew the importance of this perspective. That's why He instructed us as to how to pray and whom to pray to. He knew how critical it is for us to remain in a state of sonship, warning that "unless you are converted and become as little children, you will by no means enter the kingdom of heaven." (Matthew 18:3, ESV) Our religious minds interpret this statement to mean we are to be naturally innocent and have no guile. But that's religious thinking inspired by a religious spirit. If you doubt me, go hang out in an elementary schoolyard and observe the little kids. You'll be shocked at the meanness and selfishness you will encounter.

What Jesus was saying is that unless we convert from a religious relationship with God to the family relationship with the Father, we cannot enter the Kingdom.

What Jesus was saying is that unless we convert from a religious relationship with God to the family relationship with the Father, we cannot enter the Kingdom. A servant can never rest like a child can. A child with good, loving parents is carefree. He does not worry about getting regular meals even though he knows he may not have been particularly obedient or displayed the best character. The thought never even enters his mind. However, a servant (or employee) of even a good master (or employer) will always consciously or subconsciously be concerned about performance to feel a sense of security. Their goal is always to please in order to obtain that security, whereas a child trusts in the powerful family bond and genetic identity. That identity as a member of the family assures them that their parents' love is far less conditional than that of an employer. Even better, Jesus cleared the way for totally unconditional love—the agape love of the Father.

As I said earlier, the spirit of religion is probably the greatest enemy of mankind because it attacks the whole Church constantly and has done so for centuries. It has been especially effective at subverting our understanding of God's unconditional love for us by convincing us we need to do good things to merit more love from our Father. As Scripture says, "There is a way that seems right to a man, but its end is the way of death." (Proverbs 14:12) The religious spirit tells us to go after God's love, a legitimately good thing, but in illegitimate ways of works and self-effort. This is in opposition to simply accepting by faith that we have the perfect love of the Father through Christ's sacrifice.

I call this *pirate* activity—going after legitimate (genuine) treasure in illegitimate ways. This self-effort to please God *seems so right*, but it does not produce the results we hoped for or the life of faith that pleases God. It leads to the ultimate failure, also referred to as death.

This "death" spoken of in the above verse has broader meaning than we may think. The words *life* and *death* in this context speak to more than living or ceasing to live. *Life* speaks to the capacity for positive growth (physical, emotional, spiritual, etc.), and in this context, death speaks to the opposite.

Our goals and actions may be outwardly good, but with the wrong understanding and motive, they will not produce the life-giving fruit of the Spirit.

The ways of the flesh can be so subtle and difficult to detect because they can appear great and may even produce some good results. But from God's perspective, if the method or motive is amiss, they will be burnt up on the day of judgment and unrewarded.

So much Church activity is driven by an intention to please the Lord from a performance mindset or even from pride as we strive to build our religious trophies. We do so many things in our own power or even with a subtle mindset of fear that they become works of the flesh. Only when we encounter a problem do we seek God's guidance. God considered David a man after His heart. David never lost a battle yet still never failed to ask Him for direction before going into any battle.

Our goals and actions may be outwardly good, but with the wrong understanding and motive, they will not produce the life-giving fruit of the Spirit. If it is not of the Spirit, it produces little of true spiritual value to the one doing it. As a result, God in His mercy and love will often move through a person to whom He has given gifts to bless others; however, if that person is, in fact, operating like a pirate, he or she will not personally experience the benefits and blessings.

And what is behind those hidden mindsets of fear that turns our activity into works of the flesh? A powerful verse went over my head for many years. I read it but just did not get the connection: "There is no fear in love; but perfect love casts out fear, because fear involves torment. But he who fears has not been made perfect in love." (1 John 5:18 NKJV) I used to think this verse meant that the better I loved others, the less fear I would experience. But there seemed no logical connection as to how that worked. Was it because I would make God happier if I loved better and not have to fear His punishment? Or would He withhold blessing from me if I were not loving? It left me feeling a sense of low-level condemnation as my mind recalled my weaknesses and failures and led me to a sense of disqualification.

What this verse actually means is so freeing that it took quite a while for it to sink in. What the Father accomplished through sending

Jesus to redeem us was to permanently wash away all sin—past, present, and future, so what remains is only perfect, never-changing, complete love *from the Father towards us.*

This truth is difficult for us to comprehend because unconditional love does not come naturally to us. Therefore, our human minds tend to slip back into the enemy's subtle, tormenting accusations which produce more doubt and fear. Our accuser tells us that this or that weakness or failure is displeasing to God, so God will withhold blessing as a form of punishment until you fix it. As a result, we often pray without confidence, not expecting to get an answer, because we think we do not deserve it.

Note that Satan's accusations are not only against you but also against God. Both identities get distorted. God is accused of withholding His love and blessing based on your character and performance, and you are accused of not measuring up, even though, through Christ, you have been declared to have *the* righteousness of God and be pure in His sight.

We have been led to believe God is perfect and loves us (which is correct), and that He is sin-conscious and primarily focused on building our character. I will address this more in chapter 11, but note for now that character is the fruit of the Spirit and not something you can produce to please Him. We bear fruit effortlessly when we stay connected to the Vine.

The reality is that it's not easy to become more intimate with a God who is not so excited about you because of your issues. You are led to believe that He will always love you yet will often have a reason not to like you so much. But God does not see you that way! The extent that you think He does simply demonstrates how the religious mind has been manipulated by the enemy to accuse both God and you.

God created man in His own image and likeness. We got our emotions because we are His likeness. Before Adam fell to Satan's temptation, he walked and talked with God daily. That fellowship was lost. Also, man's dominion over the earth was lost. Literally, everything was cursed, ultimately resulting in death. God sent Jesus to fix it all, but there was a primary mission on God's mind, and this will be made clear by Jesus in the next chapter.

A GOD OF RESTORATION AND FREEDOM

If a religious person were given the opportunity to advise Jesus on the best Scripture to recite in the synagogue on the day He read from the scrolls of Isaiah 61, they would have probably chosen something focused on the holiness of God. But look at what Jesus read and concluded by saying, "Today this Scripture is fulfilled in your hearing":

> The Spirit of the Lord is upon Me, Because He has anointed Me to preach to the poor; He has sent Me to heal the brokenhearted, to proclaim liberty to the captives and recovery of sight to the blind, to set at liberty those who are oppressed; To proclaim the acceptable year of the Lord. (Luke 4:18-19, 21 NKJV)

Satan is the ultimate taskmaster, as we can see in the parallel of the Israelites' slavery to Pharoah. He hates freedom! He hates how free grace and righteousness were provided for us. He despises when our eyes are opened and we are able to accept it and access all that God has for us. The religious mind has been trained to focus primarily on God as being a holy God. He certainly is, and we should never lose sight of this! However, we are led to believe that our holiness is God's primary focus, which is far from the truth. God does desire us to be holy and already made us holy when we accepted Christ's sacrifice for our

My friend, God is not sin-focused; neither does He look down on you when you stumble and fall.

sin. As we walk in this understanding and rest in His love, He is able to reveal our failures and weaknesses and lead us into healing and restoration by His grace.

Reflecting on the verse above, we see He is a God of liberty! My friend, God is not sin-focused; neither does He look down on you when you stumble and fall. Why else would He say He has removed our sin as far as the east is from the west? He wants to set us free from sin, give us abundant life, and fill our hearts with joy.

How many times have you given or received Christmas cards that said, *Joy to the World?* Yet most Christians are not walking in any real sense of joy. We experience real joy when we truly understand the love and simplicity of the Gospel.

Chapter 6

THE PRIMARY MISSION OF JESUS

I t is one of the most misunderstood realities in Christianity today: the mission of Jesus. Why did He ultimately come?

The first thing Christians tend to think considering Jesus' mission is John 3:16: "God so loved the world that He gave His one and only Son, that whoever believes in Him should not perish but have eternal life."(NIV) That verse has become popular because it is concise and seems to point primarily to one important aspect of Jesus' mission—salvation from sin's consequences. Don't misunderstand me, Christ's atoning death, by which He took our punishment for sin and placed His righteousness on us, must not be diminished in any way. His sacrifice secures eternal life for those who believe.

But in talking with many Christians, the subconscious focus seems to be on securing salvation for us so we don't perish. We hear so many Christians talking predominantly about saving souls. I was on a road trip recently and saw so many billboards and signs with the message, *Jesus Saves!* This is very true, and thank God He does! But was that the Father's primary end? Is that why Jesus came then, to keep us from dying and get us into heaven someday?

And what do God's final words in the Old Testament (Malachi 4: 5-6) reveal about the mission of the second person of the Godhead? Why did he share that cryptic message about turning hearts of children back to fathers then go silent for over 400 hundred years before the advent of Christ?

As I hinted earlier, there is something deeper at work here.

RECONCILED TO THE FATHER

Many or even most of the serious problems we face in society today have a common factor: *fatherlessness*. By fatherlessness I mean growing up without having the healthy involvement of a loving and caring father in one's life. The evident results of our fatherlessness problem are numerous: persons incarcerated in the prison system, teenage pregnancies, addictions, high school dropouts, and poverty in general in our society.

I could write pages of exact statistics and quotations citing endless references to support my claim that fatherlessness is a significant problem today, but I don't think it necessary because it is such common knowledge. Suffice it to say, the facts are alarming. Children who have not had the experience of growing up with a caring, nurturing father are far less likely to develop a healthy identity. Without that strong sense of self-esteem, they are less likely to grow up to be responsible, sociable adults.

We are all naturally wired to need fathers! So if God intended our earthly fathers to have such a powerful impact on the most significant aspects of our lives, how much more does our heavenly Father desire to do so by personally fathering us?

As the ultimate master of strategy, God's brilliance knows no limits. His wisdom and ways infinitely surpass those of any other created being, physical or spiritual. However, at the very core of His trinitarian being, God is first and foremost relational. He exists in a unified relationship within the Godhead. Similarly, He created us to engage in a relationship with Him as a father. Relationships run on love. God *is* love. Love is relational. God is relational.

This fatherly love focus points to the primary mission of Jesus. Once again, I challenge every Christian to dig deeper regarding His mission, beginning with John 3:16. The well-known verse begins, "*God so loved* the World that *He gave….*"

The first thing to note is the motivation for Jesus' coming. It begins with the Father who "gave" His Son. In fact, the Bible usually says *God sent* Jesus as opposed to saying *Jesus came.* The Father's personal, deep desire and longing to be in active fellowship with each and every one of us motivated Him to *give* His only Son. We so often view God as emotionless, instead being emotional and passionate as we see throughout Scripture. Yet our own emotions come from being created in His image.

The Apostle Paul in Galatians gives what I call an expanded version of John 3:16 as it truly expresses in more detail what is only alluded to in John's Gospel:

> But when the right time came, *God sent* His Son, born of a woman, subject to the law. God sent Him to buy freedom for us who were slaves to the law, *so that He could adopt us as His very own children.* And because we are His children, God sent the Spirit of His Son into our hearts, prompting us to call out, "Abba Father." *Now you are no longer a slave but God's own child.* And since you are His child, God has made you His heir. (Galatians 4:4-7 NLT, *emphasis added*)

Here we see again that God the Father was motivated to send Jesus, just as John said. But now we see more clearly the purpose for doing so. As significant as it is, our redemption was not the end in itself but a means to an end. He came while the Law and the Old Covenant was still the rule of life and was Himself under the Law. He fulfilled the requirement of the law for us all for *this* purpose: so His Father can become our Father through adoption which His sacrifice made possible. Yes, salvation was very necessary because we were condemned by the Law to perish, but salvation itself was not the ultimate motivation. The ultimate motivation was to restore *intimate fellowship between us and the Father.*

I can never express enough gratitude for what my Lord and Savior did for me. The depth of His sacrifice is beyond our understanding and has enormous ramifications for our lives as Jesus continues to do His work in, for, and through us. All authority has been given to Him and it is through Him that we can and will take back dominion here on Earth. I'll revisit some aspects of this in a later chapter, but for now, my focus remains on seeing clearly Jesus' most significant mission—our reconciliation to the Father.

BIBLICAL REFERENCES TO HIS PRIMARY MISSION

John opens his Gospel account in Chapter 1 with profound statements about who Jesus is. Very early, he gives the first indication of a reason for His coming: "But as many as received Him, to them He gave the right *to become children of God,* to those who believe in His name." (John 1:12 NKJV, *emphasis added*)

Being as relational as He is, God did not send Jesus only to keep hell from filling up. That was merely the necessary first step to bring us home. We see this reality further explained in an interesting passage later in John. I've heard these words of Jesus misused so often from pulpits and in songs of old. They're usually interpreted as having to do with the second coming of Christ and having "mansions" when we get to heaven. First, let's see the context set in John 13:36-38 and then the words of Jesus in John 14:2-6:

Simon Peter said to Him, "Lord, where are you going?"

Jesus answered him, "Where I am going you cannot follow Me now, but you shall follow Me afterward."

Peter said to Him, "Lord, why can I not follow you now." (John 13:36-37 NKJV)

[Jesus said,] "Let not your heart be troubled; you believe in God, believe also in Me. In My Father's house are many mansions; if it were not so, I would have told you. I go to prepare a place for you. And if I go and prepare a place for you, I will come again and receive you to Myself; that where I am, there you may be also. And where I go you know, and the way you know."

Then Thomas said to Him, "Lord, we do not know where you are going, and how can we know the way?"

Jesus said to them, "I am the way, the truth, and the life. No one comes to the Father except through me." (John 14:2-6 NKJV)

There is much to digest here. To begin with, I am certain these verses are not related to the second coming of Christ or about having a mansion in heaven. In the last verse in the text, Jesus sums up what the entire passage is about: *The way to the Father.*

First, let's put the passages in context. Jesus and His disciples were at the last supper when He was revealing the significance of His death which was to happen the very next day. He knew this, but His disciples did not. He was about to replace the Passover lamb which temporarily covered sin with Himself, the Lamb of God. This Lamb would wash away sin once and for all by meeting the full requirements of the Law for all who believe in Him.

Jesus knew He was going to His death, and, in so doing, He knew He was going to Hell to snatch the keys that kept mankind imprisoned. This imprisonment to sin barred us from ever entering eternal life, but, even more significantly, barred us from ever becoming *children* of God. The disciples did not understand any of this as Jesus continued to cloak His life-changing truth.

Where He was about to go, they could not follow. He was not referring to His future ascension into heaven or His second coming. He was referring to what they were talking about, what was about to happen that would leave them shattered and confused. That is why He says, "Let not your hearts be troubled."

Now, in this context, let's revisit what He continued to say. Jesus chooses to use the context of *His Father* and His *Father's house*. The idea of there being many mansions in His Father's house means there is ample room for everyone, not merely to squeeze into, but to live a high quality of life as if living in a mansion—an obvious, massive upgrade. But there is no evidence in the text that this upgrade would be delayed until after His second coming. He is referring to the reality of what His resurrection would accomplish *right away*.

Jesus is basically saying this: *When I return from Hell with the keys to eternal life, I will give you immediate access to become My brothers and sisters and live in relationship with our Father as the King's children.* This understanding is further confirmed in John 20:17 when Mary first sees

Jesus on resurrection day and He says, "Go instead to My brothers and tell them, 'I am ascending to My Father *and your Father*, to My God *and your God.*'" (John 20:17 NIV, *emphasis added*)

Through His death, Jesus had immediately prepared a place for us to enter as a child in relationship with our Father. This also meant access to upgraded lives (full righteousness, provision, power, authority, healing, wisdom, etc.). Upon His resurrection and as the Way to the Father, He takes those who believe in Him into *their* household. This is what He meant when He said, "Where I am, there you may be also." He's not referring to heaven or some future event yet to happen, but to the reality we all live in *right now* following His resurrection.

This passage seems to have gone over the heads of most believers. As a result, we do not really see ourselves as Jesus' true brothers and sisters. We do not believe we are loved by the Father the *same* as Jesus is loved by the Father, and therefore, we do not have the faith of Jesus.

THE WAY OR THE DESTINATION?

To fully understand the mission of Jesus, we must address a challenging point. It may even sound like blasphemy at first to some because it challenges so much of what we have been taught in modern Christianity. So I pray even now that the Holy Spirit will give me the wisdom to make His message clear and that you will have your eyes opened to the truth and only the truth. Amen!

Satan is a master deceiver who constantly seeks to distort the Word, God's identity, and ours. One of his most successful methods is to mix a generous helping of truth with a little bit of subtle but potent lies

Satan is a master deceiver who constantly seeks to distort the Word, God's identity, and ours. One of his most successful methods is to mix a generous helping of truth with a little bit of subtle but potent lies. Yes, he will use a lot of truth, as long as the lies accomplish his deceptive goals.

Here is the point: I have observed for decades a trend within the Church—at services, in sermons, in songs, in just about everything Christian—to place the *sole* focus on Jesus. This is where one may think I'm sounding blasphemous, but please hear me out. By no means do I mean to understate who Jesus is. I understand the significance of Jesus as God, the Second Person of the Trinity. He is King of Kings, He is my Lord, my Savior, and it is His Spirit that lives in me. Without Him, I can do nothing. I can go on and on—I need and love Jesus dearly!

Nevertheless, I do not believe that God sent Jesus so that the Father can now step back into the shadows. Yet that is where His Church has put the Father—into the shadows. Yes, we mention the Father from time to time, enough to believe we have the right perspective. But the evidence reveals that we still live like servants, not sons and daughters of the Most High. Recently, my daughters attended a church meeting where the speaker's message was to say that the Father's role is to point us to Jesus—a complete flip from what the Bible compellingly states and a perspective that certainly will affect how we relate with God.

As human beings, we are created and wired to have strong healthy relationships with our fathers. Through these personal healthy relationships, we discover a healthy self-identity that shapes us into loving, wise, and confident adults. Most earthly fathers want this for their children. How much more is it God's intention to engagingly father His own beloved children! This is also revealed in John 15:1 when Jesus said, "I am the true vine, and My Father is the gardner." (NIV) He explains that it is actually the Father who is actively involved in our lives. Oh, how we tend to miss this!

Over the years, I have heard many Christians say we each have a hole in our hearts that only Christ can fill. What I have come to understand from Scripture is that when we believe who Jesus is and what He has done for us and profess our faith in Him as our Savior and Lord, He sends His Holy Spirit to dwell in us and empower us among other things. But what really fills that hole in our hearts is the love of our heavenly Abba Father ("Daddy") when we rest in finally being safely home.

To be candid, as I came into this clearer understanding of the modern Church mindset and of the utmost significance of an intimate relationship with the Father, I felt like I was entering a scary place. I say that because it felt unfamiliar to almost everything I see and hear today. Up to that point, it seemed like everything in Christianity was supposed to be about Jesus only. Yes, we all claim to be God's sons and daughters but not with the fuller understanding Jesus points to constantly.

EVIDENCE OF A PROBLEM

This time of personal reprogramming began around 2012. It caused some concern within me that maybe I was drifting off course because it seemed as if no one else was talking about this. As God deepened this revelation in my heart, I tried to find worship music to aid in my relationship with the Father. To my surprise, I couldn't find songs that spoke to this most precious relationship except for an old Maranatha album titled *Abba*.

Now you may say, "But, Colin, the Psalms constantly tell us to worship and praise the Lord!" I am certainly not saying that you should not! He is worthy of praise, and the disciples did so from time to time. However, we also need to put the Psalms into perspective.

They were written when we did not yet have the right to become God's children. (John 1:12) No one called Him "Father" before Christ opened the door. (I explain this more clearly in Chapter 9.) As a matter of fact, and to my surprise, as I did a study in this regard, I discovered that the New Testament more frequently points to worshipping the Father. I encourage you to do a search yourself. My favorite verse of Scripture in this regard speaks volumes: "A time is coming when the true worshippers will worship the Father in spirit and in truth; for the Father is seeking such to worship Him." (John 4:23 NKJV) This time is *now*!

The absence of Father focused music spoke volumes! It confirmed what I was coming to understand was a deficiency in the Church that hindered our understanding of the significant role Father God plays in our personal lives. The Church has taken a truth, excluded others, and now finds itself out of balance and unable to function properly.

Fortunately, some years later, in addition to finding overwhelming Scripture to confirm my conclusions, songs began appearing on the scene, such as *Good Good Father* (Chris Tomlin) and *No Longer Slaves* (Bethel Music). Now, the trend is rapidly growing. I now hear song after song speaking to this Father/child relationship with God and our true identity. Other recent songs include *Home* (Dante Bowe), *Real Thing* (Dante Bowe), *Run To The Father* (Cody Carnes), *Who You Say I Am* (Hillsong) and *Rest* (Kari Jobe).

When we focus solely on our relationship with Jesus, it is difficult to recognize something significant is missing

I encourage you to listen to them. Without a doubt, I believe God is laying the foundation for a new reformation—the revealing of the sons and daughters of God!

When we focus solely on our relationship with Jesus, it is difficult to recognize something significant is missing. What makes it even more difficult is the fact that everything we are doing in itself is probably right, but it is not the whole truth. What affects our spiritual health is not only what we are doing, but what we are failing to do. Of course, Jesus deserves praise and worship. He is all we believe He is. Apart from Him, we can do nothing. But take note, it is Jesus who seeks to lead us into relationship with the Father by example and revelation. The Gospels are filled, and I do mean filled, with accounts of Jesus Himself pointing us to the Father as His primary mission on earth. As you become more aware of it, you will wonder, *How did I miss this? It's everywhere!*

LISTEN TO JESUS!

When God gave His final revelation four hundred years prior to the coming of Jesus about turning the hearts of fathers to their children and children to their fathers, it was like He said, "*Let that resonate for a while!*" Those final words alluded to Jesus' future mission to reconcile us to the Father, and as we'll see, there is ample, compelling Scriptural evidence from Jesus Himself about His mission. In fact, once you realize how dominant this Father-centric message is, prepare to be surprised as you begin seeing from a different perspective and finding many other examples on your own.

Jesus almost always refers to God as *Father* throughout the Gospels. He could have referred to Him as Almighty God, Yahweh, or a host of other appropriate names, but He intentionally and repeatedly, over and over and over, referred to Him as Father. Why do we seem to take that lightly? Do we simply just see it as Him talking of *their* Father/Son relationship that is unique only to them?

In Matthew 6: 6-9, Jesus makes some clear statements about exactly who we are to pray to:

> But you, when you pray, go into your room, and when you have shut your door, pray *to your Father*....
>
> And when you pray, do not use vain repetition as the heathen do. For they think they will be heard for their many words. Therefore do not be like them. *For your Father knows the things you have need of before you ask Him.* In this manner, therefore, pray:
>
> *Our Father* in heaven.... (NKJV, *emphasis added*)

Clearly, we are to pray to *our Father* who is deeply interested and *involved* in every aspect of our lives. Let's take it a step further. The following text really rocked me as I was coming to understand how determined Jesus was to point us to engage the Father *directly* because of the deep love the Father has toward us:

> And in that day, you will *ask Me nothing.* Most assuredly, I say to you, *whatever you ask the Father in My name He will give to you.* These things I have spoken to you in figurative language, but the time is coming when I will no longer speak to you in figurative language but *I will tell you plainly about the Father.*
>
> In that day you will ask in My name, and *I do not say to you that I shall pray the Father for you;* for *the Father Himself loves you....* (John 16:23, 25-27 NKJV, *emphasis added*)

The above verses undeniably show Jesus pointing us to communicating directly with the Father when we pray. As our mediator, Jesus opened the way to the Father. However, He also makes it clear He is not mediating our communication with the Father. The price He paid to provide the way to the Father, to open the door to the household and family of God, was horrendous. How it must pain Him today to see how confused many of His people still are as to the level of intimate relationship they could have with their Father.

Understanding our identity as God's beloved child takes us to a level of faith beyond what most experience today.

JESUS SUMMARIZES HIS MISSION

Jesus said something interesting in His final prayer as He was coming to the end of His mission. He is about to face the sacrificial death which was the means to accomplish His end goal. His sacrifice would destroy our condemnation and open the door to His Father's house and our sonship. As His daily ministry of teaching was ending, this is what He says to the Father:

> Father, the hour has come. Glorify your Son *so He can give back glory to you*. For you have given Him authority over everyone. He gives eternal life to each one you have given Him. And this is *the way* to have eternal life—to *know* You, the only true God and Jesus Christ, the one *You sent* to the earth. I brought glory *to You* here on earth by *completing the work You gave Me to do....I have revealed You* to the ones You gave Me from this world. (John 17:1-4 & 6 NLT, *emphasis added*)

Jesus is saying quite clearly that the Father sent Him *to reveal the Father*. However, we have made this John 17 prayer all about Church unity and missed the primary message. Most of His prayer speaks to Jesus' unity of sonship with the Father that He wants us to also experience.

Also, consider how Jesus concludes the prayer:

> You are My righteous Father, but *the unbelieving world has never known You* in the perfect way that I know You! [*the perfect father/son relationship*] And all those who believe in Me also know that You sent Me [*the Father's initiated action*]!

> I have revealed to them [*Jesus' primary mission*] who You are [*as Father*]—and *I will continue to make You even more real to them* [*He still continues this primary mission*], so that they may experience the same endless love You have for Me, for Your love will now live in them [*unconditional perfect love of the Father*], even as I live in them. (John 17: 25-26 TPT, *emphasis added*)

Jesus clearly concludes the prayer expressing His primary purpose to reveal the Father and His commitment to continue doing so, so that we may enjoy the same father/child relationship He Himself enjoyed.

Without this understanding, we read John 3:16 with a limited perspective of just salvation from hell and little more. Besides reconciliation with the Father, we also miss another significant purpose for Jesus coming—to give us eternal life.

ETERNAL LIFE

There are many who do not understand the real meaning of eternal life. In fact, many believers think eternal life simply means life without end or living in heaven forever after death. If eternal life only referred to life never ending, then those without eternal life would cease to exist after death. However, we do know that one may never enter eternal life *and* will continue to exist without heaven, so, eternal life is not just life without end. It means much more than that.

When Adam sinned, death came in, and we also lost dominion over the Earth. We lost our spiritual authority over everything. Jesus' sacrifice immediately opened the door to restoring all that Adam lost. But, in order to experience this reality, we must understand it and act on it in faith. Eternal life through Christ restores our authority in the spiritual dimension of life, outside the earthly realm of time and space and the limits of human existence. It is a life not limited by natural power, natural authority, or natural circumstances. Yes, it is life without end, but it also refers significantly to the quality of that life since we are now seated with Christ in *heavenly* places: "(God) raised us up together, and made us sit together in the heavenly places in Christ Jesus." (Ephesians 2:6 NKJV)

We immediately step into eternal life when we receive Jesus. This reality is what is meant when the Scriptures speak of our being seated with Christ in heavenly places. Through Him, we have authority over all the power of the enemy. (Luke 10:19 NKJV) It is what Jesus meant when He said He came to give life, and life more abundantly. It's eternal life!

As Jesus said, we should pray, "Your Kingdom come, Your will be done on earth as it is in heaven." From our new eternal position, we now have the authority to bring Kingdom (eternal) dynamics into the earthly temporal and natural realm with our words that now have authority in the heavenly realm. We release angels to act to produce things that otherwise could not happen, what we often refer to as miracles.

I have chosen to focus on what I believe is first and foremost God's motivation for sending Jesus—to establish us as His sons and daughters and have everlasting real fellowship with us. In order to achieve this, Jesus had to remove our sin by paying the price for us. All authority has been given to Jesus as He sits at the right hand of the Father, and we are now seated with Him. This resets what Adam has lost—our dominion over the earth.

Hopefully, the three chapters in this section *Who is God...Really!* have enlightened you about who God really is and sorted out some of the false religion and confusion that has misrepresented Him. Let us now continue the journey and examine who we have become as the Church, how we got here, and ultimately, who *we* are—really!

Section Three

WHO ARE WE?

Chapter 7

THE CHURCH: BATTLESHIP OR CRUISE SHIP?

If you have read this far, I assume you are coming to see some of the reasons why the Church has been in an anemic state and why the Kingdom of darkness has been advancing its agenda throughout the world. This sad state has occurred in spite of there being no shortage of churches, particularly in western societies. Especially in America, there are churches everywhere, yet we find our values so blatantly eroded that we have become more of a subculture than the counterculture we were meant to be. Even worse, we are literally being shoved out by people with an antichrist spirit!

The Church can be compared to one of two radically different types of ships—an aircraft carrier or a cruise ship. I believe this comparison was first inspired by Doug Spada, the founder and CEO of WorkLife. I once served with him on the board of the International Coalition of Workplace Ministries and must give credit to him for his insightful original analogy. I have built upon his general comparisons and added my own thoughts.

THE AIRCRAFT CARRIER CHURCH

- No passengers. All signed up to serve as soldiers. They are loyal to their country (in this case, God's Kingdom) and committed to its mission and to each other.

- The primary purpose of the ship is to project power usually beyond its national waters and the ship itself, in order to take authority over an area or region if necessary (in the case of the Church, beyond its walls and into the world).

- The ship provides training and equipping of its soldiers with the greater mission always in mind.

- The soldiers (in this case pilots) leave the ship fully equipped to fulfill their unique and specific missions beyond the ship, usually deep behind enemy lines. Their individual missions usually include destroying the enemy's offensive and defensive installations and anything that threatens their nation's interests, safety, and wellbeing.

- All aspects of the ship must be maintained and cared for by its soldiers, but the ship and its activities are the means to an end and not the end in themselves.

- The captain's goals include all of the above, with a primary focus of carrying out the missions of the Commander-in-Chief.

THE CRUISE SHIP CHURCH

- The main focus of the captain and crew is the ship and its passengers. They're not very interested in anything happening beyond the ship unless it threatens a smooth trip for the ship itself.

- The major goal is to attract more passengers and keep them comfortable and happy.

- They compete with other cruise lines by ensuring they provide similar or better amenities to build loyalty and high occupancy.

- The ship is usually on a weekly schedule of repetitive activity.

- They make it a priority to stay in calm waters as much as possible to avoid rocking the boat.

- Passengers disembark at foreign ports for a short excursion (often called a mission trip by the church) but return to the comfort, routines, and activities on the ship to enjoy being fed by the crew.

- In many cases, they encourage passengers to spend as much money on the ship as possible to keep the cruise line in business and growing.

The above comparison is neither intended to be comprehensive nor to provide all of the key attributes of either type of ship. It is also not intended to offend anyone, but to be brutally honest about what the modern church has become. When the rulers and citizens of a nation see a battleship or aircraft carrier of an opposing nation enter their territory, concern, fear, and panic spread throughout the land. A cruise ship does not get the same reaction nor instill any sense of fear. The same applies to how the church is perceived in the spiritual realm. The enemy says of the cruise ship church, "Paul I know; Jesus I know, but who are you?"

EQUIPPING THE SAINTS

An aircraft carrier is a great analogy because the purpose of an aircraft carrier is to project power on behalf of a nation (Kingdom) into an area harassed or controlled by a potential enemy. This power projection is achieved by the sheer threat of its weapons, particularly its jets that can launch from the ship and attack deep within enemy territory. Each jet is flown by a pilot with a mission beyond the ship. The parallel here is that the mission of a local church is to equip God's people to fulfill their purpose and destiny, usually beyond the ship, for the advancement of God's Kingdom. "And He gave some to be apostles, some prophets, some evangelists, and some pastors and teachers, *for the equipping of the saints for the work of ministry*, for the edifying of the body of Christ." (Ephesians 4:11-12 NKJV, *emphasis added*)

Unfortunately, in our modern cruise ship church, we have developed a limited understanding of what ministry is. I am not merely talking about what the leaders do at the church or the corporate initiatives they develop for the local church body, but the unique destiny that God intended for each of us. Whether that calling is to be a mechanic, pastor, banker, or contractor, we can bring the Kingdom of God into that sphere of influence. We can start by removing the religious, unbiblical divide of *spiritual* versus *secular* so that people move boldly to take those seven mountains of culture I described earlier in this book as legitimate spiritual pursuits and reshape our culture.

Jesus said we are the salt of the earth. It is God who controls the salt shaker and scatters us throughout society by placing unique talents and passions that drive us into different areas of life. Yet the vast majority of churches place great emphasis on the activities of the local church or the functioning of spiritual gifts in a meeting setting as *the ministry*. However, what that verse says is that God gave those leadership functions to equip His people with

Why do we place so much spiritual emphasis on church-related activities and treat what we do for most of our waking hours as insignificant with no real spiritual value?

the knowledge, faith, and confidence to go into all the world, mostly beyond the church buildings, and bring His Kingdom influence and rule into all walks of life. When we think of "Go into all the world", we have been programmed to think primarily of geographic nations. But it also means going into all spheres of society, because that is where much of the world's activities take place and where we spend most of our prime time each day.

Too many believers think they are not doing anything meaningful for God unless they are on some church committee and attending church events and meetings multiple times a week. Why do we place so much spiritual emphasis on church-related activities and treat what we do for most of our waking hours as insignificant with no real spiritual value? Again, it's because for centuries we have taught the unbiblical concept of separating everything we do into one of two categories: either *spiritual* or *secular*. It is further reinforced by the words *clergy* and *laity* (also not biblically founded) to make a clear separation of those we should consider to be Men of God and the sheep. This distinction does not come from the mind of God, so you can guess where it comes from!

William Wilberforce, a renowned British politician of the eighteenth century, had a deeply personal experience with Christ during his political career. Because of that experience, he thought that the better and more honorable way he could serve God was to leave politics and join the clergy. A group of his close colleagues challenged his thinking, saying that he could, in fact, serve God more in politics than as a member of the clergy. Fortunately, he heeded the wise counsel and went on to be the person primarily responsible for the abolition of slavery in England.

If you are walking in what God created you for, it is as significant and as spiritual to God as anything else could possibly be.

How many of us miss our true calling or treat it as secular out of ignorance? How many of us would have berated Joseph for accepting the role of second to Pharaoh in the pagan land of Egypt? What about Daniel serving as a political advisor to Nebuchadnezzar? God places gifts, talents, wisdom, and understanding to do countless things the Church has called secular. Read about Bezazel (Exodus 36:1) who was anointed with talents and skills for the various work needed to build the temple.

If you are walking in what God created you for, it is as significant and as spiritual to God as anything else could possibly be. I believe this distortion of calling and purpose was inspired by the enemy to give the vast majority within the Church the feeling that only a select few were called to anything significant or meaningful to God while the rest of us have to get by as sheep. With this thinking, we cannot be a threat to Satan's Kingdom.

Consider the following verse as it ties together the desire of our hearts with our destinies: *May He grant you according to your heart's desire, and fulfill all your purpose.* (Psalms 20:4 NKJV) God puts desires in our hearts to drive us towards the reason He created us. Some people have desires for business, computer programming, the arts and creativity, serving as a pastor, etc. It is this variety that causes the world to be so diverse, creative, and advanced. It is why we have inventions in science, engineering, and medicine as well as such amazing creativity in the areas of arts and entertainment. Even though many of these areas have been predominantly controlled by the enemy, that does not contradict my point. Actually, it reinforces it. It shows why the enemy has sought to control these significant areas. Just look at what we are experiencing today because of his control of our courts, education, media, and other key influencers of society.

Our religious systems have sought to elevate the roles of what is referred to as clergy because of religious unbiblical thinking too often driven by pride, insecurity, the desire to control, and even greed. It is one of the ways Satan has deceived the masses within the Church into setting low personal expectations and being dependent on others in leadership to direct their lives. The role of leaders in the Church is to equip and coach God's people to stand firmly and confidently in their identity and authority and learn to hear God for themselves. Jesus said, "My sheep hear My voice." Directly. Can you imagine a child only able to hear from his father through someone else? Seriously, think how absurd that would be! Yet that is the sad state of a lot of people on the cruise ship churches today.

I am by no means discounting the necessity for leadership and seeking counsel. However, Satan has helped develop a religious system to discourage the Body of Christ from rising up. Yet God is awakening the sleeping giant!

What has God placed in your heart? What comes naturally to you? What do you consider your sweet spot? Unless your desire is negative, destructive, or contrary to the principles of God, it is probably God leading you to pursue your calling. God's callings are never toward mediocrity. If you desire to be in politics, business, medicine, entertainment, church leadership, media, homemaking, or education, pursue it with the understanding that God needs His people to influence these critical areas that shape our culture.

There has been an awakening to this topic in the last decade which some term as *marketplace* or *workplace ministry*. There are many good books written on the topic by authors such as Os Hillman and Doug Spada. However, it has now become an even deeper concern. Not only do we see the Church struggling as a subculture, but we are also experiencing a violent attack on our values. If we continue on this course, the stage is being set for deep persecution.

SKELETON LEADERSHIP

Because of this established separation of clergy and laity, we have developed a model of what we call *church*. How we view church is actually quite different from how Paul described gatherings of the Church in 1 Corinthians 12 and 14. To go into detail would take another entire chapter, so I recommend you read the chapters for yourself. The existing church model that can be observed throughout the Church almost globally is one that has been adopted from the Greek culture. Back then, the Greek culture focused on knowledge, not faith and relationship. Likewise, our meeting rooms today are usually set up theater-style with an audience facing an orator on an elevated platform. These orators (known as ministers and preachers) are usually chosen from a small leadership team. As they deliver a message or teaching, there is usually no interaction allowed to take place within the congregation during the service.

We should strive to encourage and facilitate both drawing out and constantly exercising the gifts given to everyone so we each can develop and function in the fullness God intended.

Paul has made it quite clear that the Holy Spirit has given gifts to everyone for the necessary edification of the Body. It is not the role of a handful of leaders to provide all that the Body needs, but to provide the right leadership to facilitate the gifts the Holy Spirit placed within the congregation to be exercised horizontally—one to another. "When you come together, each of you has a psalm, has a teaching, has a tongue, has a revelation, has an interpretation. Let all things be done for edification." (1 Corinthians 14:26 NKJV)

Churches ought to have what can best be described as *skeleton leadership*. I am not referring to minimal leadership. We are the Body of Christ, and Paul makes it clear that it is Jesus who is the head of His body, not the elders of a church. Jesus had a human body with an internal skeleton, not an exoskeleton (like that of a crab). The skeleton provides the necessary structure internally to facilitate the development, growth, and movement of the body, but it is not meant to be all that is seen. We should strive to encourage and facilitate both drawing out and constantly exercising the gifts given to everyone so we each can develop and function in the fullness God intended.

While I am on the topic of leadership, I must address the use of titles, though I stress I am not seeking to offend or dishonor anyone. We are at a time when ignoring unhealthy practices would be amiss. The title situation has become quite toxic. In the church today, we are expected to address or refer to anyone in church leadership as Pastor Tom, Bishop John, or Apostle Harry (in cruise ship lingo, Captain Tom, First Officer John, etc.). Should I then introduce myself as CEO or Chairman Colin since I have a business? Is that what I require of my employees? Of course not. After speaking at a meeting of Church leaders once, I was approached by an arrogant man who introduced himself as Apostle Prophet John Doe (not his real name). He handed me a card that had so many titles and letters before and after his name that it literally filled two complete lines. I felt sick. He said he really would like me to contact him. I have to admit, the card never made it home.

I know this is an extreme case, but why is it Paul, Peter, John, and even Jesus are called only by their names, but not so with His servants today? Are we so insecure in our calling that we must be separated from and elevated above the rest of God's people? Or is it pride? This practice only serves to perpetuate the unbiblical separation of *secular* and *spiritual, clergy,* and *laity.*

SPIRITUAL AUTHORITY

As I said at the beginning of this book, when I came to Christ, I immediately told Him I needed to see His relevance in business, where I spent my prime time. Soon after, I began experiencing deep challenges that caused my faith to be tested. I began experiencing God and the miraculous so profoundly within the realm of business that I felt compelled to motivate others to experience the same. God wants us to understand how heaven and the whole spirit realm see us and to exercise our authority to bring His Kingdom dynamics into our sphere of influence, whether working in a restaurant or bank, as an accountant, nurse, or stay-at-home parent.

We have been taught to think that only the pastors have the spiritual authority, but in fact, believers who work in the city and, even more so, those who have businesses in the business district of the city, are the spiritual leaders of that business district.

When we truly understand our identity, we wield a level of spiritual authority that will release angels to work and send devils fleeing. You may say, "But I am just a server in a restaurant!" It doesn't matter what position you hold if you have a clear understanding of who you are.

Understanding this spiritual authority is vital. I began in 2005 to mobilize Christians in the business district of our capital city, realizing that if we are Christians established in the city, we have the spiritual authority to impact the city. We have been taught to think that only the pastors have the spiritual authority, but in fact, believers who work in the city and, even more so, those who have businesses in the business district of the city, are the spiritual leaders of that business district. They need to exercise their authority to release God's influence.

I began bringing together hundreds of Christians who work in the city to weekly pray for the city on Wednesdays at noon in the City Hall auditorium. The idea was to shift the typical religious thinking by having such meetings in the middle of the workweek, in the middle of the day, and in the middle of the city. The City Hall, where the mayor's office was, represented the seat of political power.

At that time, I also felt led to mobilize all of the Christian denominations to gather for a day of united prayer along with the Global Day of Prayer movement. Uniting all of the different denominations together like this had never been done before in Trinidad and Tobago, but I believed God wanted to use our group of businesspeople to make it happen. I was the president of the Christian Chamber of Commerce at the time and used our non-denominational status to pull them together from a neutral, less-threatening position. We also had the know-how to do an effective media blitz and manage every aspect of the undertaking.

I met for prayer with a small group of intercessors. I asked the Lord to show us how to pray. Understanding how principalities operate, I asked Him to reveal the enemy's stronghold in the city that hindered us spiritually from achieving success in these endeavors. He revealed through one of the intercessors that the stronghold was a section of the city where illicit activities such as drug dealing, prostitution, and other crimes were rampant.

We thought we might go to the site with a small inconspicuous group of three and walk through the area quietly praying to break the stronghold of the enemy over our city. However, one of the intercessors felt the Lord warn us not to step foot in there but to pray and declare the stronghold broken right from where we were. We did so. Two weeks later, I awoke to the news that the entire city block where the stronghold was had been burned to the ground by a raging fire the night before. Not a single business next to it was damaged! No buildings within the area where these illicit activities were taking place survived, and yet nothing beyond was damaged. There was also no loss of life or injuries.

A few weeks later, we held our large national prayer event in a stadium-like venue in the city with representatives and leaders of every Christian denomination. It was a time of humbling of ourselves and repentance for the nation. There were many bishops and church leaders present, but no one had titles that day. No one wore religious garb. There were no distinctions between clergy and laity. As all denominational differences were laid aside, the only one exalted that day was Jesus Christ. It was one of the most moving events I've ever experienced. It was a resounding success and was covered positively on the front pages of the national newspapers. God shifted something that day on a national spiritual level.

Why am I sharing this? I am doing so to challenge you to understand not only how heaven sees you, but also how the enemy sees you when you are confident of your identity. I encourage you to expect much more for your own life. In the book of Judges chapter 6, we read the story of Gideon. When he was approached by the angel, he was fearfully hiding from his enemies and considered himself as one from the lowest family that belonged to the lowest tribe of Israel. That was the understanding within the social system of Israel at the time. It was who his world told him he was. However, in Judges 6:12, the angel greeted him this way: "The Lord is with you, you mighty man of valor!" (NKJV) Heaven saw him differently. Gideon eventually allowed God to manifest this reality in his life.

ANOTHER SHIP

As you may recall, I shared a vision an intercessor sent me where she saw me jumping overboard from a pirate ship. She said I was walking the plank trying to escape groups of people who were after me to get involved in their ministries and organizations. Then she said the Lord appeared and told me to jump off the ship because He was about to do something different with me. The Lord said it was going to be just between Him and me alone. It completely resonated within my spirit, so I left everything and metaphorically jumped off the pirate ship and into Iowa.

There is a third ship that best represents a way of thinking and functioning within the Church today. It is that ship I refer to as the pirate ship. And understanding the analogy is key to making sense of what we see in the church today.

Chapter 8

THE PIRATE SHIP

In this season of shaking, the times we are in require us to allow God to shake everything within us. He wants to shake loose things that have been poorly constructed. Such shaking is usually not pleasant.

The thoughts that I shared in the last chapter, and those I am about to share in this one, are some more reasons why the Church is so ineffective today. Unless we are prepared to recognize them and admit that we have to change, we will remain stuck on the same track we have been on for a long time. I hate to have to refer to the already overused definition for insanity, but we cannot continue doing what we have been doing and expect to see different results. I do not believe revival will come simply by wishful thinking without some form of reformation within the Church—reformation in how we understand the pure Gospel and the methods we employ when we deviate from it.

You may recall from earlier my story of the intercessor's vision of my jumping from a pirate ship. The vision was given when I was visiting a prophet friend named Johnny Enlow. He had asked one of his intercessors to pray for me. She saw it while praying even though she had never met me. After discussing the vision, Johnny said to me, "Do you realize she said 'pirate ship'? Pirates go after legitimate treasure in illegitimate ways."

That statement has turned out to be the most revealing and profound statement to describe so much of what is going on in our churches and ministries today.

I want to be very clear, I am not referring to illegal activity within the Church, but to the extent that the Church has been operating in the ways of natural man and not by the Spirit. There is so much going on that is not of the Spirit or faith. But because we are getting some results, we assume God is in it and blessing it.

We read in Matthew chapter 14 of how Jesus fed the five thousand with just five loaves of bread and a couple of fish. He made everyone sit and receive through the direction and movement of the Spirit. I'm not trying to say that whenever we want to achieve, we should sit and do nothing. However, I do suspect the way this problem may have been handled if left to Jesus' disciples would have been through a committee that would mobilize fundraising efforts with teams to solicit donations in every nearby village. If it were today, we probably would hire a team of professional media experts to bombard the Internet with social media posts compelling people to give, using techniques I cannot imagine Jesus using if they were available to Him. And yes, there would be some results.

There is a subtle but significant principle here. I say subtle because it is not so easy to detect. There are many things we do daily in life that are amoral—they are neither right nor wrong (like choosing what mug to drink from). However, when it comes to things of spiritual significance, God wants them done by faith and the Spirit's leading. The ways of natural man are not usually of the Spirit's leading, and while they may be legal and socially acceptable, by God's standards they may even be considered sin. Romans 14:23 tells us that "whatever is not from faith is sin." (NKJV)

Our tendency is first to use any resources and acceptable methods we have available to us as a natural default. Then when we face challenges, we go to God to get us over the obstacles or meet the shortfall. Our actions may not appear to be a matter of right or wrong, but are they guided by the Spirit or the flesh? Anything outside of the Spirit's ways is technically illegitimate in God's eyes, even if we are getting results. We may have good intentions and seek to build His Kingdom, seeking legitimate treasure, but we're going about it in illegitimate ways.

We all, from time to time, fall into pirate activity because of our human nature. But simply because millions of us fall into this weakness should we shrug our shoulders and continue? If we do not recognize how far we have drifted, we cannot hope for and imagine something different.

Let's face it—twelve relatively poor and insignificant men turned the whole known world upside down two thousand years ago without a single institution, but today, even with billions of dollars spent on ministry and with all of the structure, education, and effort, we are still struggling to keep our culture from perpetually sliding downward.

It has been my observation that many ministries today have built huge institutions with complex administrative structures at high financial costs that operate no differently from what we call secular organizations. Many of these large institutions find themselves trapped within a complex system they are now compelled to maintain with little thought as to whether the Holy Spirit is in it. And yet these ministries become the goal and standard the small ministries seek to emulate.

Some food for thought: During Jesus' years of ministry, did He reveal or demonstrate, even once, a focus on establishing the type of institutions that exist today, or any institution for that matter? I am not saying no institutions should exist. I am simply pointing to the natural human tendency to build and control them. If these organizations are developed in the flesh, they anchor us down to countless stressful activities that keep us from being loose and flexible to move as God leads.

Let's face it—twelve relatively poor and insignificant men turned the whole known world upside down two thousand years ago without a single institution, but today, even with billions of dollars spent on ministry and with all of the structure, education, and effort, we are still struggling to keep our culture from perpetually sliding downward. We need to admit that the Kingdom of darkness seems to be moving forward with little resistance. Evil seems to be growing, and for the most part, we appear weak and powerless to stop it. Something is clearly wrong!

We keep declaring that Jesus reigns and He will come through for us. That is also my hope; however, it will require that the Church get off the pirate ships and cruise ships and begin to truly function like an aircraft carrier church. We need to walk in the Spirit (which I will get into more deeply in chapter 11, and trust me, it's probably not what you think it means). Let Him build what *He* wants to build!

I am reminded of the time Jesus was transfigured on the mountain (Matthew 17: 1-5) while He met with Moses and Elijah. It seemed like Peter and the others with Him immediately wanted to institutionalize the event with the construction of tabernacles. Had Jesus allowed them to do so, we would probably be having large pilgrimages to that site to this day with countless people and resources involved in the operations. It would have been a seemingly spiritual activity yet led by the flesh.

Another time, the disciples wanted Jesus to settle in a town where He had great success healing a crowd the day before. (Luke 4:40-44) The following day, another crowd had returned, probably larger than the previous one. However, Jesus did not stay, because the Spirit was leading Him to move on. Jesus actually left people with needs and moved on. Honestly, how many of us today would walk away or even think to ask the Holy Spirit, "What would you have us do Lord? Do we continue?" Who would do that today, particularly while getting results and with people continuing to be in need of our ministry? I think almost all of us would do everything possible to keep it going without thinking otherwise. All too often, we see where God does something in our midst, and for years afterward, we try to keep it going any way we can, even though God has moved on. Could God have different plans than we do? Part of the problem is that our identity gets so wrapped up in what we are doing and our new-found service or ministry fame that we begin to claim it as our own.

It has also been my observation that there are certain predictable and concerning techniques used to pressure people into supporting a ministry. We seek to entice people to stay with us and buy our stuff with deals, sales, and freebies constantly through social media, email, and other forms of Internet technology. I am not saying that discounting something because we are overstocked or seeking to draw someone's attention to material that would help them is at all wrong, but it has almost become a standard practice to bait people. If we have to entice someone to renew a subscription or membership with freebies or deals, we should ask, "Am I really effective in reaching the hearts of these people? Is God directing me to do it this way? Is He wanting to move me on? Is the Spirit drawing people to what I have, or are they drawn to the deal or freebie?"

In the passage mentioned earlier, Jesus did not stay in a town for weeks, months, or even years until the healings became few and far between. We should not primarily do things because of a need only. We ought to act on obedience and ask, *What is the Holy Spirit saying?* Jesus obeyed the Spirit when He regularly passed the crippled man (very much in need) begging at the gate to the temple so that Peter could one day bring healing to him. (Acts 3) Honestly, this place is where many drift or become stuck.

After Jesus fed the five thousand in John 6, the next day the crowd continued to follow Him. Jesus was not tempted to try to hold onto the numbers of followers, knowing that many of them would be the fickle, freebie/deal-seeking type. As a matter of fact, He sought to turn them off intentionally, to sift out the fickle-minded ones with talk of eating His flesh and drinking His blood. It is only after they left that He clarified what was said to His disciples.

"It is the Spirit who gives life, the flesh profits nothing. The words I speak to you are spirit [lowercase s] and they are life." (John 6:63 NKJV) He clarified that the words He is speaking have a spiritual message that would give life through the working of the Holy Spirit. The flesh itself as spiritual food will gain nothing. He explained that His words earlier were not literal but speaking allegorically with spiritual meaning (as He so often did). After sifting out the crowd of uncommitted ones, Jesus looked to the remaining disciples and asked in John 6:67-68, "'Do you also want to go away?' Simon Peter answered Him, 'Lord, to whom shall we go? You have *the words of eternal life.*'" (NKJV) This is further backed up by Matthew 4:4, "Man shall not live by bread alone, *but by every word* that proceeds from the mouth of God." (NKJV)

The point is that Jesus was capable of being tempted and could have been tempted to hold on to His growing number of followers like many church and ministry leaders do today. It's all about the numbers!

This temptation is a ploy of the enemy to get us onto a pirate ship and away from fulfilling our true destiny.

HEAVEN'S REWARDS

I do believe that many will be shocked when they are facing the Lord in the end to find that, while they are certainly saved and will be lovingly welcomed into heaven, a lot of their works will not make it past that day. Instead, those works will be burnt up along with the chance for eternal rewards:

> Now if anyone builds on this foundation with gold, silver, precious stones, wood hay, straw, each one's work will become clear, for the Day will declare it, because it will be revealed by fire; and the fire will test each one's work, of what sort it is. If anyone's work which he has built on it endures, he will receive a reward. If anyone's work is burned, he will suffer loss; but he himself will be saved, yet so as through fire (1 Corinthians 3: 12-15 NKJV)

What we may be holding on to for fear of loss may actually be hindering us from fulfilling our destinies God intended and receiving His eternal rewards.

This passage of Scripture refers to our one and only chance when our works and ministry here on Earth will be tested by the fires of the Lord. Are they made of gold, silver, or precious stones? (faith) Or are they in His eyes, wood, hay, and straw that burn easily? (the ways of the flesh) Are we going to assume that because so many people are doing things a certain way that they must be right, even though we may feel a subtle conviction that there is a better way, beyond doing our own thing but requiring deeper faith and rest?

What we may be holding on to for fear of loss may actually be hindering us from fulfilling our destinies God intended and receiving His eternal rewards. Can you imagine the deep regret we could have when we discover we are entering heaven with considerably fewer rewards than we could have had? These are eternal rewards our minds can't even perceive and do not expire!

BENCHMARKS OF SPIRITUAL GROWTH

How many of God's people use natural benchmarks to judge spiritual growth and success? "I have this many more members in my church this year, so obviously God must be very pleased with my ministry." What if you have been building a cruise ship? Is God going to judge you by the number of comfortable passengers on board your cruise ship or by how effective those soldiers are on your aircraft carrier?

About fifteen years ago, as a leader in marketplace ministry in Trinidad at the time, I was asked to speak at a conference for the leadership of the largest denominational organization in the Caribbean. The topic I was given to speak on was *Go into All the World*. At first, I thought it odd that a businessman would be asked to address their leadership and be given such a topic. But then it became clear to me why God had opened that door and what He wanted me to say when an odd verse of Scripture came to mind. I had never seen it in that context before: There is one who scatters yet increases more; And there is one who withholds more than is right, But it leads to poverty. (Proverbs 13:7 NKJV)

This verse primarily speaks to giving; however, the Spirit revealed that the principle can also be applied to church growth and success. The role of the church and its leaders is to equip the saints for ministry—the ministry God has called each of them uniquely to beyond the church walls. If church leadership fails to equip them to understand their full identity and the power and authority they have been given in their sphere of influence, such a church will come to poverty. You may say, "What poverty? I have more members than last year?" Well, it depends on the criteria we use for success, and is it the same as God's? Is it about how many passengers we have on the cruise ship? Or, is it about how effective the jets have been in fulfilling their missions off of the battleship?

If you want to know how successful your church is, I encourage you to conduct two surveys. One is amongst the membership with questions like this: Do you feel spiritually valued? Do you feel you are being equipped to find and fulfill God's destiny for you beyond the church? Do you feel you are moving towards a sense of fulfillment in what God has given you a desire for and destined for you? The other survey I would conduct is in the community where the church resides. I would ask this question: If this church were to shut down, what notable or tangible impact do you think you would observe?

The church's ministry is to catch and release—catch the lost and release them into the destiny God intends for them.

If we fail to affirm our people and help the Lord scatter them beyond the ship, we may simply be managing a cruise ship in God's eyes. These people are God's. They do not belong to an institution. The church's ministry is to *catch and release*—catch the lost and release them into the destiny God intends for them. When people are equipped by a church to walk confidently with God on their own, God will keep bringing in more for training because He can trust the leadership. Leaders are meant to create conduits as opposed to building corrals. I believe this is why, in spite of the fact that we have church buildings on almost every corner, we Christians are the tail and not the head in society.

On a more personal level, what are the benchmarks we use for spiritual growth? "I just got invited to join the worship team or lead a ministry. God must be pleased with me for Him to elevate me!" Is that it? Well, I recently heard of an internationally-renowned worship leader who walked away from Christianity completely! He claims to no longer believe in God! What was his benchmark for spiritual growth? He was up on stage but spiritually weak. If you have a passion to do something, it is natural to be excited about doing it. However, it is dangerous to use ministry as a benchmark of God's love or approval.

Over the years, I have observed many within high levels of church leadership who have drifted significantly from where they began. There were times I have had to work with some of them. It was always a constant battle against the ways of man. I would often feel distraught and upset. I began thinking, *What would cause such well-respected leaders to become like this?*

I considered the likely reality that they probably all started off humble and genuine, so the shift must have been almost undetectable, like the proverbial boiled-frog effect. That left me terrified because I realized that unless the Lord protected me and led me, I would surely drift in the same direction. I was becoming very well-known in my country in the area of marketplace ministry and could see how coming into the limelight could become a temptation for pride and works of the flesh. I begged God to protect me.

A couple of years later, He asked me to jump off the pirate ship. I completely left my identity as a business leader, marketplace ministry leader, and church leader but gained my true identity as His son in a way I would have never otherwise understood.

JUST STOP!

I challenge anyone willing and able to completely stop all ministry activity in order to experience a deeper personal revelation of God's love by grace. When I arrived in Iowa, I began a journey of doing just that. The area I moved to was in a religious community, but I knew I was not supposed to just jump on board. I felt a strong sense that God wanted me to do nothing but rest in Him with my family and trust Him. It was a scary experience at times because I felt alone with the fear of drifting aimlessly away from God. I often thought, *I must be shipwrecked!* But God kept revealing and confirming His love at deeper and deeper levels.

Another thing I learned from that experience was that God knows my heart and motive for getting off the hamster wheel. He will protect and keep me because He is my Father! The best way I could describe my experience is by sharing a vision I had some years later (in 2018) that was quite clear and detailed.

In the vision, I was at a large European-style train station with many tracks. I was sitting on a bench by one of the tracks waiting for a train. A number of really large trains came into the station and one or two people got off. A large vintage train (more modern than the first steam engine type but still older) pulled in. It looked like it was probably sixty to seventy years old. It was absolutely huge and impressive, especially because it was so close to where I was sitting. I was in awe. There were thousands of people on this train heading in the same direction that all of the other trains were heading. I remember feeling that I was expected to get on the train—but I just couldn't.

I sat on the bench, remembering a previous trip on a similar train heading to the same destination. On the previous train, we were traveling through beautiful wild country like out west in

Wyoming with streams and rivers, mountains, and rugged lands with lots of fresh air. But we could only barely see through the windows because they were dirty and misty. Not many people were even trying to look out because there was a lot of activity happening on the train.

There was a deep desire in me to get off and experience the beautiful natural rugged scenery, but there was nothing I could do. The train was on a set track heading to a large, safe town, but nothing there was exciting or would feed my passion for more.

So this time, I just could not get on. I sat there on the bench thinking something must be wrong with me. There were so many other people on the train, and I was alone on the bench. Should I follow the crowd? They all seem resigned to go to where the train was taking them. But I wanted more. It was scary watching that train leave while I remained sitting on the bench.

Just then, I felt a hand on my left shoulder. I looked around to find my Father looking at me smiling. He said, "Come, son." The next moment, I was at a beach where there were a number of little sailboats with a couple of people getting onto each boat. In each pair, one person was a regular human, and the other was dressed in a white gown representing either an angel or the Holy Spirit. The Father then said to me with a smile on His face, "Trust Me." I remember excitedly but cautiously getting into the boat with a person in white. The wind immediately filled our sail, and we began sailing out to sea. It was windy and the sea was a bit choppy—yet it felt so right.

CROSS OVER!

For some of you, this was probably a difficult chapter to read. During the COVID-19 crisis, we saw special attention placed on keeping churches closed. Many see this as persecution of the Church; however, I believe God has allowed it to achieve His end—an opportunity for serious introspection. It's no longer business as usual.

He clearly wants our attention to lead us to cross over into a new era. The sleeping anemic giant needs to be awakened and strengthened for this next season. The new wine cannot be put into old wineskins. Our cruise ships need to be decommissioned or go through major refitting. The pirates need to surrender.

If you consider the train analogy, trains run on set tracks with a predetermined destination. If you believe you are on such a train heading to a destination you are not thrilled about, you need to get off. Get off the existing mindset and ask the Holy Spirit to renew your mind to His ways. He wants to switch you to a four-wheel-drive jeep, able to go anywhere off-road, beyond the paved man-made roads and religious paths.

Are we servants seeking to improve our position in the pecking order of institutions, or are we becoming confident sons and daughters led by the Spirit in all we do?

Whether it's ships or trains, it all speaks to the way we see both church and ministry and also ourselves and our spirituality. Are we servants seeking to improve our position in the pecking order of institutions, or are we becoming confident sons and daughters led by the Spirit in all we do? Are our identities and sense of value wrapped up in what we do rather than who we really are?

In Luke 8:22-25, Jesus told His disciples, "Let us cross over to the other side of the lake." (NKJV) Because He asked it, that did not mean it was without challenges. As a matter of fact, they thought they were going to drown!

We are certainly at a crossroads where God is wanting to lead us a different way. This is a time of transition. It will not be easy, but He is with us. He will guide us. We will get to the other side if we trust Him and launch out. As we do, I believe God has some amazing things planned for His transformed Church.

Chapter 9

WHO AM I...REALLY?

The seven sons of Sceva had been traveling from place to place as exorcists, according to the biblical account in Acts 19. As they observed the effectiveness and authority of Paul's ministry over devils, they attempted to cast a devil out of a man by saying to it, "We cast you out by the Jesus whom Paul preaches!"

These men appear to have had good motives; however, the devil responded, "Jesus I know, and Paul I know; but who are you?" In other words, *Who are you to command me when you do not understand Paul's authority, and what qualifies him to use it effectively?* The man in whom the evil spirit dwelt overpowered them all and beat them badly, sending them fleeing naked from the house. Paul clearly understood his true identity and authority in Christ (not because he was an apostle) and wielded it confidently.

But that is not true for most Christians. The devils know those who *get it*—and are terrified by them. They also know those who do not.

We see evidence of this uncertainty yet again in the way we pray. After listening to many Christians pray over the years, I've noticed we often begin our prayer with "Dear" followed by "Jesus", "Lord", or "Father." But think about it. The only appropriate time we would begin communicating with someone using the word *Dear* would be when formally writing to someone. Let's face it: this expression does not speak of the close, relaxed, (but, of course, respectful) and personal relationship children usually have with their parents who live in the same household.

There's another word used frequently in prayer by just about every Christian in the western world today. It's the word *just*. Listen to anyone pray—including yourself!—and see if you can get through a single prayer without the word *just*. I challenge you to try. Unless you are consciously stopping yourself, you'll likely find it almost impossible! Try to avoid it, and you may sound like a cell phone call with a weak signal, stopping and starting awkwardly as you try not to say it.

You may be thinking, *Really Colin, what's the big deal with using the word "just" when we pray?* Well, words are powerful. God used them to create all things. They also reveal where we are spiritually. Both He and the enemy hear the words we use when we pray. When we say "Dear Lord, we *just* ask......" what we are really saying is: *We don't want to bother you; we only want...; We don't want to ask for much, just this...; We hope you are okay with...; If you're not too busy we only need....* It means we are not coming to Him with confidence nor full knowledge of the relationship we should have with Him.

Now, I know we all do it, and many are doing it out of sheer habit; for others, it's false humility and religious lingo. Not only is it unnecessary, but it is also quite the opposite of how the Father wants us to approach Him—confident and genuine!

Think about it. What if your child approached you and said, "*Dear* Father/Mother, thank you for all the meals you provided in the past, but... but, I *just* want to ask for one more thing... and *just* that... if only I could *just* get that. Thank you! Thank you!" You would probably stand there speechless, disappointed, confused, and even hurt. After all, it is not presumptuous for a child in a healthy family relationship to expect his parents to meet his needs and direct his life for success. Because of what Christ has done, we are children in a healthy family relationship and should confidently expect our Father to do the same for us and even more.

But even when we speak of what Christ has done, we reveal a misunderstanding of who we are in relationship with God. Have you ever heard anyone say, *Because of what Jesus did for me, when the Father looks at me, He sees the blood of Jesus?* It's as if Jesus provides cover for that person to hide behind. That thinking perpetuates the lack of confidence to come boldly to your Father and betrays an ongoing sense of shame and identity confusion.

Because of His sacrifice, all who believe now have the righteousness of God—not merely a pinch of it, but all of it!

While that statement may sound like praise for what Jesus did, it is unbiblical and far from the truth. It paints a picture of a dirty, unloved child hiding behind the perfect, favorite Son (Jesus) and peeping out timidly at the Father. But that is far from the reality of what Jesus accomplished for us. Because of His sacrifice, all who believe now have *the* righteousness of God—not merely a pinch of it, but *all* of it! Jesus was the first of what is now a large family of beautiful, righteous children of the Father.

I believe a lot of this orphan thinking comes from misunderstanding the work of Jesus' blood. Christians everywhere often use the phrase "covered by the blood of Jesus." We cover our families, our businesses, and just about anything we want protected with the blood of Jesus.

While there may be no real harm in the statement itself, I think it has led many to use it carelessly, reinforcing weak thinking of what Jesus in fact did with our sin.

Jesus does not *cover* our sin! After the first sin of Adam, God used the skin of an animal to cover Adam and Eve's nakedness. The first blood was shed for sin. Right up to the death of Christ, the blood of sacrificial animals continued to temporarily cover man's sin. When something is covered, it is hidden, not removed. Hence, they needed to regularly offer the blood of animals to constantly renew that temporary cover the Law provided. This also served to remind the Israelites of their sinful state and the need to look forward to the promised redeemer.

That's why it was such a big deal when John the Baptist declared, "Behold! The Lamb of God who *takes away* the sin of the world!" (John 1:29 NKJV, *emphasis added*) The time for merely covering sin was nearing an end. At the shedding of Jesus' blood, sin was finally *removed* for all who believe! A study of the Bible will reveal many passages reiterating this very thing. Our sin is now removed. In God's eyes, we are now sinless because Christ paid for it all. Plain and simple.

As Paul says, "He made Him who knew no sin to be sin for us, that we might become the righteousness of God in Him." (2 Corinthians 5:21, NKJV) He does not say we have a portion of God's righteousness. We are seen by God to have the same righteousness as Jesus: "For God knew His people in advance, and He chose them *to become like His Son, so that His Son would be the firstborn among many brothers and sisters.*" (Romans 8:29 NLT, *emphasis added*)

The bottom line is this: As the Father looks at me, He sees me and delights in me, Colin, as His unique and beloved son, a sinless brother of Jesus, because of my simple faith and full acceptance that Jesus took away my sin once and for all 2,000 years ago.

GREATER THAN JOHN THE BAPTIST?

The Gospel of Luke tells us of the time when John the Baptist was imprisoned and sent a message to Jesus asking if He was truly *The* One. In the latter part of Jesus' answer, He makes a revealing statement: "Amongst those born of women there is not a greater prophet than John the Baptist, but he who is least in the Kingdom of God is greater than he." (Luke 7:28, NKJV)

I've often wondered, how could the least in the Kingdom be greater than John the Baptist and other prophets like Moses, Jeremiah, and Elijah, just to name a few? These were powerful spiritual men used by God to do profound things like parting the Red Sea and calling down fire from heaven. Yet the least in the Kingdom is greater than all of them? How is that possible?

It begins to make sense when we recall that up until Christ's redemption, man was separated from God and relied on the blood of animals to temporarily cover sin. But those sacrifices could not bring anyone into sonship—a true Father/child relationship with God. Until Christ came, there was no way to be adopted into God's own family, to be accepted as a legitimate child of God the Father. "But as many as received Him [Jesus], *to them He gave the right to become the children of God*, to those who believe in His name." (John 1:12, *emphasis added*)

The redeemed child has had his sins removed and has been fully adopted into God's own family, a position that was not possible for anyone before Christ!

We see this distinction when reading the Old Testament. All of the prophets, including those I mentioned above, usually addressed God as *Lord* but never as *Father*. Even David, who was considered a man after God's own heart, did not refer to God as his Father. I love reading the Psalms, and I draw tremendous encouragement, insight, and direction from them; however, if I am praying a Psalm today, I often exchange *Lord* with *Father* because it is what Jesus taught me to do. I am also mindful that I am now in a much greater relational position with God than David was when he wrote it. I am now also seated with Christ in a position of authority over the spirit realm that the prophets of old simply did not have.

I believe this current reality is what Jesus meant when He said the least in the Kingdom (even a recently redeemed sinner with a checkered past and no works of ministry under his belt) was greater than the renowned prophets of the Old Testament. The redeemed child has had his sins removed and has been fully adopted into God's own family, a position that was not possible for anyone before Christ! The Bible is not a bag of random verses of Scripture we pull from but must be read and understood in proper context.

WHAT HAPPENS WHEN I SIN?

Most Christians struggle to understand that Jesus' sacrifice paid for all their sin—once and for all—and removed it as far as the east is from the west. (Psalm 103:12) This truth has profound ramifications for us even as it raises questions such as, "What happens when we do sin? Are we then no longer sinless?"

When we repent and accept by faith Christ's sacrifice for our sin, we are born again and have become a *new* creation, not simply a covered version of the same person. Our old man has been considered crucified with Christ so all requirements for fulfilling the law have been met by Jesus. God gives us a brand new spirit that is *permanently* in right standing with Him. I used to think that if I sinned after becoming born again, my new spirit would begin to become soiled all over again. I thought only by confessing again and asking for forgiveness could my spirit be cleansed and made righteous again. But if that were so, what was the purpose of our spirit becoming a completely new creation?

Jesus said, "Whoever has been born of God does not sin, for His seed remains in him; and he cannot sin, because he has been born of God."(1 John 3:9 NKJV) It used to be that every time I read that verse, I would feel somewhat heavy because I knew I would fail from time to time. Eventually, I began to understand how our being is made up of three separate parts—spirit, soul, and body. Only then did it begin to make sense. While they are connected, one is not the other. Our spirit is not some little spiritual space inside of us, but actually our full eternal being. Our soul is our mind and emotions that are connected to our spirit. All of this is housed in our body.

Because of advanced medical technology today, we have countless stories of people whose bodies literally died on operating tables for short periods and were then revived. Many of them explained later that they saw themselves lying on the operating table from above and heard what was going on. Have you ever wondered how they could see and hear since their physical eyes and ears were still with their bodies on the operating table? It is because our spirits are not some little spiritual space within us, but our real selves and not limited by the natural.

While our spirits are redeemed and have the ability by God's grace to overcome anything, the weakness of our flesh still exists and continues to war against our spirits.

What John is saying in the above passage is plain and simple: if you are born of God (born again) your new creation spirit simply cannot sin—even if you sin.

(I know. I can hear you screaming now: *What!?*)

If we fall into sin, it is not our new creation spirit that does so. There is a carnal side of man not yet redeemed that the Bible refers to as *the flesh*. While our spirits are redeemed and have the ability by God's grace to overcome anything, the weakness of our flesh still exists and continues to war against our spirits. When we lose sight of our real identity as a beloved son or daughter who has been washed and born again, we drift from intimacy with the Father. Fears begin to take over, and we begin to walk in the flesh, driven by these fears and lusts for counterfeits. By so doing, we wreak havoc in our lives. However, this flesh-walking does not affect our spirit, which always remains in right standing with God.

Let's consider what Paul has to say about this. I used to wonder if Paul was schizophrenic when he referred to sin and said, "But now, it is no longer I who do it, but sin that dwells in me." (Romans 7:17 NKJV) And again, "Now if I do what I do not want to do, it is no longer I who do it, but it is sin living in me that does it." (Romans 7:20 NIV)

Paul was explaining the separation between our born-again spirit and our flesh. Our new spirit will always remain in right standing with God our Father and is completely loved by Him. Therefore, we can rest in knowing we are God's beloved children, and we are always His delight, even when we may have struggles in the flesh. Satan tries to deceive us with doubt in this area precisely so we will not feel comfortable running back to God's always-open arms. (Trust me, I will bring even more clarity on this and the consequences of sin in chapter 11.)

NOT PARDONED, JUSTIFIED!

Another error I often hear Christians make, even in songs, is to state that God has pardoned us for our sins. Pardon for sin can be found numerous times in the Old Testament. However, nowhere in the New Testament does it say we have been pardoned for our sins under the new covenant. What we will find in the New Testament, however, are many verses such as Romans 3:24 stating that we are now *justified*: "Being *justified* freely by His grace through the redemption that is in Christ Jesus." (Romans 3: 24, NKJV, emphasis added)

There is a big difference between being pardoned and being justified. First, let's revisit what the Bible often refers to as the *courts of heaven*, where Satan comes to accuse us of breaking God's law or not acting in faith. In this way, he tries to disqualify us from God's favor and His intended destiny for our lives. In the old covenant, the Scriptures say God pardoned the Israelites' sin by the shedding of the blood of animals on their behalf. A pardon does not remove sin nor guilt, it only removes the penalty; therefore, the guilty verdict still remains. In the new covenant, however, Christ's sacrifice removed all sin *and* guilt. He who knew no sin took our sin on Himself and suffered the penalty to wash it away—it's all gone!

In a court of law, there are four stages in a case brought before a judge: the plea, the trial, the verdict, and finally, if found guilty, the sentence. Only *after* going through all four stages and being found guilty and sentenced by the judge can a person be pardoned. In fact, the Hebrew word for pardon means to *forgive* or *spare*. In the old covenant, the annual blood sacrifices of animals only *spared* mankind from the penalty of sin for the year. However, the guilty verdict remained unchanged.

Justification is very different. The biblical meaning in the Greek language is *to render just* or *declare innocent*. A friend who is a high-level judge in the Caribbean explained that justification is established at the very first stage in a court case—the plea. When an accusation is brought against you in the court of heaven, you are asked, "How do you plead?" Your lawyer, Jesus (or advocate as the Bible puts it), states that you are innocent. Because all sin and guilt have already been completely removed by Him, the plea is accepted. The case is instantly thrown out because the judge (God) knows anyone whom Jesus represents is already innocent. There is no trial nor verdict and, of course, no sentence. *No pardon is required.* The charge is determined to be a false accusation.

Yet I know you may be thinking, "But I know I still fall into sin from time to time!" True. However, because Jesus fulfilled the requirements of the law once and for all concerning sin on your behalf, your sin is permanently gone in the courts of heaven—taken away. You have been justified!

PROOF OF SINLESSNESS

In the Old Testament, God instructed Moses to build a tabernacle where His Presence would dwell among mankind. "And let them make Me a sanctuary, that I may dwell among them." (Exodus 25:8, NKJV) It was where the priests would go before God to offer animal blood sacrifices to temporarily pardon and cover sin.

The part of the tabernacle where God's Presence literally dwelt was called the Most Holy or the Holy of Holies and was separated from the rest of the tabernacle by a very thick curtain or veil for man's protection. Only the high priest could enter that area after following strict consecration procedures to offer sacrifices for the people. No one else could enter—period. Failure to offer sacrifices for his own sin before entering would result in his sudden death as he entered.

When Jesus died, He became the final High Priest with the ultimate sacrifice that would pay for all sin, once and for all (as confirmed throughout the book of Hebrews). At the death of Jesus, *"the veil of the temple was torn in two from top to bottom...."* (Matthew 27:51 NKJV) This Scripture reveals that we no longer need other men to offer sacrifices or represent us before God. I have heard this verse interpreted countless times to primarily mean that we are now free to boldly approach the throne of God. Yes, this is true! We are now free to do so because of the death of Christ. But, if that were the only significance of the veil tearing, wouldn't we be making pilgrimages to the same temple in Israel to go boldly before Him ourselves, no longer needing a priest to represent us?

The most significant aspect of the veil tearing open is that, as of that moment, God was no longer dwelling in a temple built by man but in those who would believe in Jesus. *"Do you not know that you are the temple of God and that the Spirit of God dwells in you?"* (1 Corinthians 3:16 NKJV)—the same Spirit that dwelt in the Ark of the Covenant and placed in the Holy of Holies!

Remember, our sin is not covered but removed, and here is simple proof of our constant sinless state: As I explained earlier, during the old covenant, sin could not be present in the Holy of Holies where God dwelt, and should a priest enter with sin, he would die. Yet with the new covenant, God dwells in you and me today. If sin were still present in us, would we not die also?

ABOUT OUR FATHER'S BUSINESS

By now, I pray you have no doubt that if you have trusted Christ, you are a beloved child of God, a brother or sister to Jesus, having His same righteousness, pure and delightful in the sight of God. I hope you also understand that if you fail, your redeemed spirit remains sinless. You may be asking, "Are there no consequences then when we sin?" Of course there are, and they can be quite grave! However, those consequences are not the punishment of God, but rather, the result of allowing the enemy access to ruin your life which I'll explain later in Chapter 11.

When I was a young man, I started working for my father in his business. There were others my father looked to for support who were older and far more experienced than I. They also held authority over many areas. Somehow, and without giving it conscious thought, I never felt threatened by their positions in the company. I was subjected to the same rules, policies, and benefits as other employees.

As I look back, I realize my primary motivation for working well was not achieving targets, performance reviews, nor fear of losing my income and benefits. I was motivated by an innate desire to be about my father's business. I desired to walk in his steps. As an employee, he was my boss. While that fact was not a conscious focus, I never really forgot because I naturally conformed to the rules and policies like everyone else. But I was a good employee because I naturally shared his interests in the business. Beyond the office, we continued to share life together because he was my dad. As his son, I was his heir and eventually did inherit the business.

The point I am making is that because of my DNA and true identity, I was motivated by his interests which also became mine. This motivation made me a good employee. I didn't focus on trying to be a good employee, and neither should we focus on being a good servant of God. Get to know your Father and live like a son, and you will naturally also be a good servant. You will love learning from your Big Brother and Lord as He guides you to follow how He does it. When people say things like, "I pray my loved one will serve the Lord," I wonder if we even grasp the amazing new life and relationship that God intends for us, of which service is only a part and will come naturally?

I suggest we pray instead that our loved ones will trust in what Christ did for them so that they can become beloved children of our heavenly Father and truly know Him in that way. If that happens, they will eventually be about their Father's business, empowered by the Spirit while living in true rest as sons and daughters of God. Living in that state is what most attracts the unbeliever.

WHAT TO DO NOW?

Chapter 10

ONLY BELIEVE

You may recall that on the day I began writing this book, President Trump declared a state of emergency in the United States because of COVID-19. By the following week, all nine stores in my optical business in Trinidad had closed as the government there mandated a lockdown that continued for two months. Our company had already experienced a huge loss the month before because of a rapid drop in consumer spending as fear began to spread. In over four decades in business, I have never experienced such an evaporation of wealth and have no idea what lies ahead.

Before the pandemic, I already faced business challenges from rapidly increasing competition due to a school of optometry that had opened in Trinidad within the last decade. On top of that, exporting oil and natural gas drives Trinidad's economy. But the price of oil had dropped eighty-five percent or more, from approximately $75 a barrel a few years ago to single digits.

To make matters even more complicated, when I left Trinidad, I had to leave my own company's pension plan at the most critical years of funding my retirement. Having never worked in the US, I do not qualify for Social Security. Raising nine kids and putting them through college is a huge draw on finances, but if I can avoid having my children start their careers with student loans, I want to make every effort to do so.

To top it all off, as a U.S citizen with business abroad, I have also fallen into a new and unusual tax law introduced in 2018. It was intended to force mega, multinational companies to pay US tax on their holdings abroad, but it has penalized small companies in the process. The law is so onerous that I have been praying God would send a foreign buyer for the business who is able to pay me in US dollars. How likely is that to happen with a business in Trinidad? Yet in 2019, out of the blue, I was approached by two international companies interested in buying the business. I experienced real hope that I could sell and secure my financial future. Then came COVID-19.

All of this is becoming like Elijah's sacrifice on Mt. Carmel. He soaked the wood several times and even surrounded the altar with a moat of water with no matches to be found. Only God could do something in that scenario. Not in my wildest imagination could I think of something so devastating to a business painstakingly built over forty-eight years. Will there be a business left to sell? Will there even be any interest to buy, as everyone now rethinks their strategies post-COVID19? I appear to be in a real pickle.

Why am I sharing all of this? I felt it would be useful to reveal my own overwhelming struggles as I write because they require me to personally process the very principles I'm talking about. Will God come through for me? Does He want to come through for me? How am I supposed to concentrate on writing at this time? Yet I am certain I must write this book now, in the midst of all these distractions. I do not believe I would know the extraordinary peace I am experiencing now if I had not come to a deeper understanding of who my Father really is and His deep, engaging love for me.

You see, faith is not as blind as people say it is. I remember way back in my late teens while hanging out with my friends, a girl was encouraging another weeping friend after her boyfriend had broken up with her. She told the sobbing girl, "Have faith! He will come back!" I remember thinking in my limited wisdom at the time, *Are you kidding? What is the basis for having such faith? That's ludicrous!* Now, that is what I call blind and wishful faith.

But such blind faith is not what God expects from us. The more we know our Father and see our magnificent identity in Him, the more we will base our faith on informed facts, not wishful presumption. This is why the Bible says faith comes by hearing, and hearing by the word of God. (Romans 10:17) God's word reveals the truth of who He is and who we are. The more we understand these truths, the more we can put our faith in Him.

The more we know our Father and see our magnificent identity in Him, the more we will base our faith on informed facts, not wishful presumption.

Imagine you are a special forces soldier in today's U.S. Army on a covert mission. You must parachute into a remote jungle in South America and make a 50-mile trek through the jungle to your target. However, you encounter a skirmish between two uncivilized tribes that have no knowledge of the outside world. A man from one tribe is trapped by a dozen men from the other tribe. You can see he has only three arrows left and is about to lose his life. Feeling pity for him, you try to signal to him that you have grenades he can throw at his opponents. Then you throw him a couple of the grenades. What do you think he would do? He would probably ignore them, thinking he prefers his three arrows to your two polished "Rocks".

If you could pause the scene, show him some informational videos and demonstrations of grenades in action on your iPhone, and then restart the scene, it would probably resume somewhat like this: On seeing the two grenades a huge smile of excitement and hope would come upon his face. He would grab the grenades, pull the pins, and launch them at his adversaries. They would grin at the stupidity of his actions *until....*

You get the picture. Do you see how a little accurate knowledge can change things? His faith was not blind, but was based on newly-found knowledge of a power beyond anything he had previously known. On that knowledge, he could act with confidence.

When based on the right knowledge, faith is actually highly logical. It makes sense to trust God.

WHAT IS FAITH, REALLY?

To truly understand faith, we need to consider the opposite—*fear*. Faith is the absence of fear. A simple example may help us understand the distinction.

When I was freshly out of high school, I took a job at an air-conditioning company assembling window air-conditioning units. As part of my training, I learned how air conditioning works. It does not actually produce cold air, but rather removes heat from the air instead. Cold is not something in and of itself. It is simply the absence of heat. Heat is the known entity; however, cold is simply less heat. Yes, if you stand in front of an air conditioner, you'll feel cold air blowing at you, but that cold air is actually produced

> *If we can remove all fear from our minds by becoming aware of the full truth of God's love for us, all that will be left is faith.*

when room temperature air is sucked through an extraction system, heat is absorbed and removed, and the colder air blown back into the room.

In the same way, if we can remove all fear from our minds by becoming aware of the full truth of God's love for us, all that will be left is faith. This simple but powerful understanding of faith reveals how to develop it. If you can identify the fear behind your concerns (doubt, disbelief, condemnation, identity confusion, etc.) and find the opposing truth, your fears will dissipate, leaving only faith.

However, in the midst of challenges and tribulations, we often seek to stand on faith by declaring verses of Scripture about faith without intentionally going the extra step to identify the opposing fears and reject them. This is why the Bible says to "bring every thought into captivity to the obedience of Christ", (2 Corinthians 10:5 NKJV) and "whatever things are true...meditate on these things." (Philippians 4:4-8 NKJV) This one-sided effort can bring only a short-lived measure of success because we do not really understand that faith is the absence of fear. Instead, we try to pile faith on top of fears without removing the fears themselves.

God moves when we pay Him in the currency of heaven—faith. He is compelled to do so because it pleases Him most. "But without faith, it is impossible to please Him...." (Hebrews 11:6a NKJV) Thus, He seeks children of faith so He can reveal Himself to and through them. "For the eyes of the Lord run to and fro throughout the whole earth to show Himself strong on behalf of those whose heart is loyal to Him." (2 Chronicles 16:9 NKJV) This loyalty is not to performance but to His message of faith. God showing Himself strong on our behalf means miracles, power, and wisdom beyond our natural limitations.

GOD'S PERFECT LOVE

As I mentioned previously, I had always struggled to understand 1 John 4:18: "There is no fear in love; but perfect love casts out fear, because fear involves torment. But he who fears has not been made perfect in love." (1 John 4:18 NKJV) My religiously-trained mind felt condemnation (which I mistook for conviction). I presumed it was because I was not demonstrating enough love to others. I thought if I loved more, I would have less to fear. And besides, how could I ever perfect my love? I usually felt failure and subtle condemnation after reading that verse.

Yet this understanding is far from the truth! What the verse really means is this: When we grasp how perfect God's love is toward us because of Jesus, the Lamb that fully and permanently removed all our sin, we need never fear we are not good enough to be loved by the Father always. He will not withhold any good thing from us who believe.

If we consider all that we have covered, we should understand by now that many in the modern Church do not truly understand the primary mission of Jesus. His primary mission was to make a way for our adoption as sons and daughters, not for our recruitment as servants. Certainly, we are serving in a powerful army fighting with authority and power through Jesus Christ our King and Lord. But effective power and authority come through a clear sense of our true identity.

It was not God's intent for us to simply find a friend in Jesus and then put our entire focus on living for Jesus. That would be like an adopted orphan, after being brought home, camping out at the doorway and connecting only, for the most part, with his new sibling. But the brother alone cannot provide a confident sense of sonship. For the orphan to fully understand his sonship and have a relationship with his father is what would best drive away any fears of not being loved and looked after by his new father.

He would also feel comfortable to enter the house and enjoy it all, not simply linger in the foyer.

For the most part, too many Christians don't truly understand that in becoming born again, a new spirit is placed in us that cannot sin; therefore, we permanently have the righteousness of God ourselves. It is why we are encouraged to walk in the Spirit, in that new identity, so fear cannot creep in through accusations that challenge reality.

Because of the completeness of Jesus' work on the cross, God will always delight in us with complete, total, ongoing love. This is perfect love.

You see, 1 John 4:18 is not speaking of our love, but of God's perfect love (through grace and grace only) that places us in such a sinless state and of being a delight to Him. Because of the completeness of Jesus' work on the cross, God will always delight in us with complete, total, ongoing love. This is perfect love. We must walk in this understanding that nothing can separate us from such love.

The fear and torment this verse talks about refers to what we experience when we do not understand our sonship. Often, we do not feel confident that God completely accepts and loves us as we are. Instead, we tend to listen to the lies that tell us God won't answer our prayers because our ducks do not line up in a row the way He wants to see them.

We either consciously or subconsciously feel that God withholds the answers to our prayers as a subtle punishment for our poor character.

Because of the enemy's accusations, we subconsciously feel we do not deserve to be blessed. This torment is what the verse speaks about.

Other translations of the verse put it a little differently saying, "[B]ecause fear has to do with punishment." (1 John 4:18 NIV)

Understand that God, as a loving Father, may not release a blessing or answer a prayer because He knows best what is good for us. We may be asking for the wrong thing or the timing may not be right. But rest assured that He will reveal in time how He had your best interest at heart. If you trust His love, you will one day thank Him for how He worked it out for your good. The key phrase here is "trust His love."

The bottom line is this: We either consciously or subconsciously feel that God withholds the answers to our prayers as a subtle punishment for our poor character.

This distortion comes from the spirit of religion which says that God is holy and therefore always sin-focused, and besides, "Don't be ridiculous! Blessing and favor can't be that free!" At this point, we are to tell the enemy to shut up as we continue to walk in the Spirit. God delights in this confidence and faith for it is what abiding in Him really means.

So, as I write these words in the midst of the perfect storm of apparent hopelessness regarding my financial future, I completely rest in this: I know who my Father is. I know how much He delights in me. And I know He's got this!

I have had the most delightful times as a dad with eight of my nine kids home with me during the COVID-19 lockdown. No one has whined about being stuck at home, and the weather has been gorgeous. We've spent hours together just sitting, resting, and laughing on our southern front porch. We have all experienced an amazing peace that really does surpass understanding.

SIMPLY FAITH

Have you heard this popular statement, "God helps those who help themselves?" Many people believe this statement is scriptural. It is not. In fact, the basic message of the Gospel is quite the opposite. The Old Covenant was based on the obedience of man to observe all that was written in the law and, in so doing, God promised to bless him in all manner of life. However, the New Covenant is quite different in that it promises not just blessings in our temporal life, but also the removal of sin and the ability to enter eternal life itself. In short, it promises us sonship.

Most significant is that it is not based on performance but faith only. The Old Covenant, as we see throughout the book of Deuteronomy, was temporal. It promised a better quality of life here on earth. It was based on God saying, "If you..., I will....". The New Covenant is very different. It says, "I will... only believe!" Simply faith.

Because of our sinful nature, the Old Covenant was impossible to fulfill. Because of our naturally religious minds, the New Covenant can often seem too easy to accept. Yet it is abundantly clear:

- "God so loved the world that He gave His only begotten Son, that whosoever *believes* in Him, shall not perish but have everlasting life." (John 3:16 NKJV, *emphasis added*)

- "As soon as Jesus heard the word that was spoken, He said to the ruler of the synagogue, 'Do not be afraid; *only believe.*'" (Mark 5:36, *emphasis added*)

- "Then they said to Him, 'What shall we do that we may work the works of God?' Jesus answered and said to them, 'This is the work of God, that you *believe in Him* whom He sent.'" (John 6:28 & 29 NKJV, *emphasis added*)

How often do we just pass over this significant word *believe* not grasping the weight of the instruction? The word *believe* is at the very core of the Gospel, and we call it Good News. There is nothing we need to or can add to what Jesus did. The New Covenant operates by faith and faith only. Simply but factually stated, anything else rejects the Gospel.

In *The Faith That Works*, Peter Youngren brought to light an interesting fact: there were only two people whom Jesus referred to as having *great* faith. One was the Roman Centurion (in Matthew 8:10) and the other was a Canaanite woman. (Matthew 15: 22-28) The thing they both had in common was that neither of them was Jewish. They knew they were not Jews and did not follow any of the law's requirements. According to

Believing we can earn God's favor by our faithful performance is actually sin.

Jewish laws and customs, they would be the least capable of qualifying for any of God's blessings. Thus, they approached God purely on the basis of who He was and what He was capable of, knowing quite well they deserved nothing.

So many of us approach God hoping for an answer to prayer based on our goodness or Christian performance. We (often subconsciously) think He should bless us because we are a worship leader, an usher, faithful volunteer for children's ministry, a pastor, etc. This thinking is the same as the elder son in the parable of the prodigal. It is servant thinking, not born of understanding sonship, simple faith, or grace.

Believing we can earn God's favor by our faithful performance is actually sin. ("For whatever is not of faith is sin...." Romans 14:23) I believe it is why Paul referred to himself as the chief of sinners. In Philippians 3: 4-6, Paul talks about his diligence to the requirements of the law. He considers himself practically the greatest sinner in this regard. He went as far as to say in verse 6 that he was blameless! How could he now say in 1 Timothy 1:15 *"That Christ Jesus came into the world to save sinners; of whom I am chief?"* (NKJV) In light of his previous boast, his statement sounds like a case of false humility and contradiction. Or was it?

Consider this: If performing good deeds, doing ministry, and making every effort to please God in order to feel a better sense of His approval is considered sin, then yes, Paul was the chief of sinners. He was certainly an expert on religious performance.

I challenged you back in chapter 8, *The Pirate Ship*, to step away from doing anything that looks like ministry. You may think I am nuts to suggest this. Most pastors would berate me for suggesting it. But do you think you could stop every form of alleged ministry activity for a minimum of six months and still feel the complete love and delight of the Father?

Don't gloss over that question. Most people will. But I dare you to stop and really consider it.

Could you stop everything other than your personal communication with God and be comfortable and confident in your relationship with Him while you did *nothing*? In my thirty-five years as a Christian, there were two times in my life when God led me into an extended period of stopping all ministry—and I mean ALL ministry. During those periods, He would not let me hold on to one remaining thing. "Just one!" I reasoned. *Nope!*

I do not think you can fully understand the effects of doing this until you actually experience it. Many people would waste no time throwing loads of Scripture at you, condemning your inactions and warning you of the dangers. Most of what they would use as scriptural examples would be made to seem like laws you should abide by if you want to maintain a good relationship with God.

DISRUPTING RELIGION

Yet during those times that I stopped *everything*, I experienced such increases in revelation, growth with God, and lessons I will never forget. When you are doing nothing for Him and allow Him to reveal how much He delights in you, what you *thought* you knew then becomes reality.

Right now as I write, many are freaking out that people can't go to their churches during this COVID-19 period of lockdowns and social distancing. Yes, I do believe the enemy is at work in this. However, I see quite clearly how God wants to use this time to reveal how dependent most believers have become on the hamster wheel of religious duty and activity. This dependency has severely diluted our ability to truly fellowship with our Father daily as His true children. What the enemy meant for evil, God is using for good to expose where we truly are. Frankly, we need this!

What the experience may also reveal is a hidden sense of insecurity and feeling unloved that we attempt to cover with religious activity, ministry, and sacrifice. For so many church-goers, these are key benchmarks of growth and acceptance. We subconsciously think, *God must be pleased with me for Him to promote me to this position of ministry!* Or, *I must be growing in maturity and knowledge beyond my peers for me to be asked to do this!* This thinking is far more prevalent than most people want to admit. It is not something to

When we are in the wrong place—whether by our activities, people we fellowship with, or even the church we attend, we become cloudy and dull in our ability to receive fresh revelation for ourselves.

dismiss because it reveals what we depend on to feel valued by God. We become just like the elder son that Jesus spoke about in the prodigal parable.

I have also come to realize that when we are in the wrong place—whether by our activities, people we fellowship with, or even the church we attend, we become cloudy and dull in our ability to receive fresh revelation for ourselves. We usually get stuck in a cycle of religious busyness but may not actually be in the perfect will of God for our lives. This effect is actually the result of the enemy's work. Many settle on the subconscious feeling that they can only really hear from God through other people. If my earthly father mostly spoke to me through one of my older siblings, I would probably be sitting in jail now or doing drugs. At the very least, I would be quite dysfunctional.

Jesus is our shepherd. He said, "My sheep hear My voice." Jesus also said at the beginning and very end of His prayer to the Father that He came to reveal the Father to us: "I have revealed to them who you are, and I will *continue* to make You *even more real* to them, so that they may experience the same endless love that You have for Me, for your love will now live in them, even as I live in them." (John 17:26 TPT, *emphasis added*)

In this unusual season, I believe God wants to develop our ability to hear the voice of Jesus shepherding us towards the Father and to hear the Father directly speaking to us, His children. However, in order to develop this, we will need to leap by faith into our Father's perfect love for us. It will require *only* faith and no more! *Only believe!* Without such essential faith, we cannot please God. However, in order to have such faith, we must identify our fears and displace them with the truth about who He truly is and who we truly are.

Stop sweating it out, my friend. Step off the performance hamster wheel. God wants you to enter true rest. He wants to love on you—as you are.

Chapter 11

WALK IN THE SPIRIT

W hat does it mean to walk in the Spirit? Based on the responses I get when I ask that question, it appears just about every believer struggles to give a confident answer. I find most people are uncomfortable with the question, not only because they lack a clear answer but also because they have a gut feeling they are not doing it well. Thoughts come to mind of needing to pray and meditate more, lose their temper less, or maybe pray in tongues or just stay silent and listen for the voice of the Spirit. In general, they feel the need to live a more holy life.

Having a strong expectation of what I would find, I searched the Internet to hear what others say walking in the Spirit means. I discovered a lot of vague generalizations and somewhat misappropriated truths. Here are a couple of perspectives I discovered online:

- "So walking in the Spirit is a God-consciousness. It's having Christ foremost in all your affections. It's pursuing God with all your heart as we are commanded to."

- "The way we abide in Jesus is to be practicing what we call the spiritual disciplines ... things like, Bible reading, Bible memorization, Bible meditation, prayer, fellowship, church attendance, evangelism and serving other people. These are the ways we abide in Jesus."

Sounds kind of right, yes? While a lot of those are good and necessary Christian activities, they are not the primary criteria to walk in the Spirit. They are many of the things we all should engage in as we seek to understand and follow Christ, but they do not speak specifically to the term *walk in the Spirit.* Their predominant message usually is that to walk in the Spirit, you need to either be in longer and deeper meditation or practicing the so-called disciplines of Christianity more ardently. Their message is basically this: Performance equals walking in the things of God. This thinking often results in a sense of condemnation and a loss of joy.

It is not my desire simply to criticize but to open up what I believe to be one of the typically misunderstood truths in the Bible. Instead of condemning, it actually is encouraging, refreshing, and liberating.

In a previous chapter, I explained that God gave us a completely new spirit, which is why Jesus referred to us as being born again. Our old spirit-man was considered crucified with Christ. The old spirit-man is gone. We have been reborn. According to 1 John 3:9, our new spirit *cannot* sin because the Father's seed (of righteousness and sonship) *remains* in us. I also showed in Romans 7:17 and 20 where Paul clarified *twice* that when he does the opposite of what is right (sin), it is *not him*, the redeemed born-again spirit he now is, but the flesh where sin takes place. (Fear not! I am going to address sin and its effects further in this chapter.)

When a Christian does not understand what really happens when born again, they live with a lot of confusion. Because of this separation between the spirit and the flesh, we are now in perfect standing with God our Father through Jesus Christ. We have been given His righteousness so we are now flawless and blameless. His love is perfect and constant towards us. You cannot and do not keep switching in and out of this state of love when you fail! It's simply mind-boggling what Jesus has done for us! I encourage you to listen to these two songs that speak to this: "Flawless" by MercyMe, and "Blameless" by Dara Maclean.

When the enemy attacks this truth, he intends for us to doubt our new reborn state in God's eyes. I stress *in God's eyes* because we can't see it in the natural realm. He attacks the core of what it means to walk in the Spirit. To walk in the Spirit means to walk confidently in the belief of our new spirit identity, in-dwelt and empowered by the Holy Spirit. This reality is what the Spirit has made possible with our spirits. We need to walk in this knowledge and awareness. Doing so has tremendous power to overcome sin, as I will explain.

Satan hates it when we are full of faith and confidence in our relationship with God. Thus, he subtly yet effectively accuses us to create doubt about our new state in Christ. We begin to doubt God's perfect love and unchanging acceptance of us, allowing fear to creep in. We lose confidence that He will come through for us because we no longer feel deserving of His blessing. We then tend to drift away from God and into the works of the flesh. "I say then; Walk in the Spirit and you shall not fulfill the lust of the flesh." (Galatians 5:16, NKJV)

THE WORKS OF THE FLESH

In Galatians 5: 19-21, Paul gives a partial list of these works of the flesh: "Adultery, fornication, uncleanness, lewdness, idolatry, sorcery, hatred, contentions, jealousies, outbursts of wrath, selfish ambitions, dissensions, heresies, envy, murders, drunkenness, revelries and the like...." (NKJV) All of them can be traced back to fear. We begin to walk in our own strength, striving in different ways to obtain satisfaction through counterfeits, control and manipulation, and other even more evil activities.

These works of the flesh (sin) have serious consequences. However, if by believing in Christ our sin is paid for and taken away, what then are the consequences of sin when we *do* fail? When we consider the works of the flesh above, we can easily see how we would reap damaged relationships, sickness (even death), financial crises and poverty, harmful addictions, perverted minds, and a host of other very negative things if we walked in them. We allow the enemy access into our lives and reap the consequences.

God desires that we walk with the awareness of His love and delight in us because it counteracts the pull toward such things. It is also why Jesus urges us to abide in Him, to remain firmly in all He has done to make us beloved children of the Father, and to allow His grace to work in us. When we do this, we experience rest and peace that allows the fruit of the Spirit to bear. Jesus said so simply: "I am the vine, you are the branches. He who abides in Me, and I in him, bears much fruit; for without Me you can do nothing." (John 15:5 NKJV)

THE FRUIT OF THE SPIRIT

But many of us still struggle when it comes to the fruit of the Spirit. In Galatians 5:22, Paul reveals the fruit of the Spirit: love, joy, peace, patience, kindness, goodness, faithfulness, gentleness, and self-control. Our religious minds tell us that since we do not measure up, we need to be more disciplined and do better. We think it is the Holy Spirit convicting us of our poor state. The Holy Spirit does convict us of our failures, but usually in a way that produces a sense of hope through a faith solution. But I ask you candidly, do you usually read that verse and feel encouraged? I never did.

What we fail to notice is they are called *fruit* of the Spirit. We cannot bear fruit by our striving. It isn't about more effort by us, but resting in the reality of a loving God doing the work to produce these fruits in His children. As we walk in the Spirit as I explained above, the non-striving conditions exist to bear fruit. It is like I explained in the previous chapter on faith. If we remove our fears, faith and peace rise. Likewise, if we cease the works of the flesh by believing in our identity and trusting the Holy Spirit, the fruit of the Spirit naturally replaces them. It is always going to be one or the other. In the absence of heat, there is cold. In the absence of fear, there is faith. In the absence of the works of the flesh, there will be the fruit of the Spirit.

As to the conviction we think we feel when reading that passage, it is probably valid. But understand that the enemy is always seeking to condemn. When we understand what it means to walk in the Spirit, we are better able to discern between conviction and condemnation. Also, think of this: We know the Holy Spirit convicts us of sin; however, He also *convicts us of righteousness*. This is important to grasp! Jesus said, "When the Holy Spirit comes, He will convict the world of sin, *and of righteousness* and of judgment." (John 16:8 NKJV, *emphasis added*) The Spirit desires to burn His conviction of righteousness (through Christ) into our hearts, so we can discern the accusations of the enemy, reject them, and rest in our new identity and position with God our Father.

I know there are many that are wondering, *But what about the discipline of God? Don't we need disciplining at times?* Certainly we do! It is the Father's way of shifting us from our folly and placing us back on a healthy path. But that healthy path begins first and foremost with right thinking. Only then will we have His grace working in us to change our actions.

Yes, the Holy Spirit certainly wants us to know when we are in sin or on the wrong path. There is no denying that. But, I do not believe it is because He is sin-focused. He wants us to have a clear and strong conviction from Him of the full righteousness we possess—*the righteousness of God*. When that conviction is clear and strong, we naturally will walk in the Spirit. As we walk in such grace and peace, He produces His fruit in us. As we remain in His rest, we lose our fear that drives our desire to control, manipulation, envy, anger, and things that lead to addictions.

Fear drives the works of the flesh, but accepting His perfect love casts out fear.

Fear drives the works of the flesh, but accepting His perfect love casts out fear. Yet for many years, I have heard the following Scripture taught with a focus on condemnation, guilt, and religious performance: "I say then; Walk in the Spirit and you shall not fulfill the lust of the flesh." (Galatians 5:16, NKJV) But, as you should now see, the reality is quite the opposite.

A PRACTICAL EXAMPLE

When I began to see truths like this one that had been wrongly taught, it blew my mind. At times, I felt it was too good to be true. I prayed that I would not fall into heresy, but God kept backing up my new understanding with Scripture. We are wired and even taught to think so differently from what the Holy Spirit intends that I think it would be helpful to give a practical and relevant example of how this works.

We live in a time where pornography is accessible with a simple click on an Internet browser. A floodgate has been opened in our society as evil has rushed into every home with the intent to fuel perversion, lust, and abuse that destroys healthy relationships and causes wide-scale, uncontrollable addiction. In addition to my two girls, I have seven boys ranging in age from 9 to 26, so this is a concrete topic for me. Regardless of filters and software to protect against pornography, we all know it is impossible to block everything. Ideally, I want my boys to have the ability to live as overcomers in spite of the onslaught. The true and lasting solution to this problem of pornography is not what many suggest.

When attempting to help people overcome an addiction to pornography, emphasis gets placed on a determination to resist temptation with strong accountability. While this sounds right to some degree, what is really needed is often misunderstood, especially in the context of walking in the Spirit.

Someone with a strong addiction to pornography often has experienced some form of emotional, physical, or sexual abuse. Such abuse usually affects the person's self-worth negatively, instilling a belief that they are unlovable and deserving of the abuse. Shame becomes the underlying emotion that tends to lead them away from God, thinking He too is disappointed and disgusted.

In this state of shame and feeling unlovable, the enemy tempts them to fill the void with pornography. Pornography is a temptation at the core of our natural being—our sexuality, which in itself has natural desires. However, it is a perverted counterfeit to real love. Now, more shame gets piled on.

After addressing any abuse with forgiveness of the offenders, and repenting from their involvement with pornography, the individual needs to understand that Christ has already paid for all of his sin. He has been in right standing with God ever since he received Christ. Not only that, but his Father truly and always sees him as His beloved son. There is no longer any shame on anyone who is in Christ. If the believer can truly accept this truth, the lies planted by the enemy no longer control his emotions. The desire for Satan's counterfeit diminishes considerably.

The next phase is to do as Paul says in Romans 12:2, "Be transformed by the renewing of your mind...." (NKJV) When we are used to certain types of thoughts, our brain develops physical protein wiring through which these thoughts flow as habits. When there is a new habitual change of thought, the brain wiring associated with the previous thoughts eventually disintegrates from lack of use as new wiring forms and strengthens to carry and store the new thought patterns. The necessary change in thought needs to be, first and foremost, how the individual views himself in his Father's eyes. He needs to train his mind to stand on God's Word and accept his true identity as the Father's beloved child, to overcome the accusations, rejection, and shame. Only then can lasting transformation develop. Walking out this truth would draw him to God, not away from Him, bringing inner healing and peace. Only then can he address the thoughts from the temptation itself. On the other hand, if his primary effort is to shove lust out of his thoughts, he will fail.

- "Whatsoever things are true, ... meditate on these things." (Philippians 4:8 NKJV)

- "Casting down arguments and every high thing that exalts itself against the knowledge of God, bringing every thought captive into the obedience of Christ." (2 Corinthians 10:5 NKJV)

- "Walk in the Spirit and you shall not fulfill the lust of the flesh." (Galatians 5:16 NKJV)

If we believe that merely disciplining oneself not to engage in pornography and holding the individual accountable is the solution to achieving lasting change, we are wrong. As Paul said, "For what I will to do, that I do not practice; but what I hate, that I do." (Romans 7:15 NKJV) He may set his *will* to do better, but he will fail miserably with a repetitive cycle of sin and repentance. Accountability may seem to reap results for a short while because of the sheer determination to avoid having to admit to embarrassing failure, but it does not last long. Usually, the person continues to fail on and off. They begin to lose hope and may even lie to their accountability partner, causing them to feel hopeless and despicable. And I am talking about Christians who feel this way!

My friend, this resetting and retraining of the mind for someone to see himself as God sees him is the key to overcoming this plague of pornography on the minds of our fathers, husbands, and sons—and for our women, as well. When we help them to walk in the Spirit, they will not fulfill the lusts of the flesh.

It is saddening how many churches today preach constant sin-consciousness with a subtle focus on guilt and shame. Once again, Satan mixes truth with lies to cause our failure. Yes, of course God hates sin, but He provided an amazing solution to deal with it. As a result, He is not sin-focused! Do you recall the prodigal's father who didn't even wait for the son to finish his confession speech? Yet for decades our religious teachings have implied (probably unintentionally) that God loves you but doesn't really like you. So clean up your act and live right! The message and method completely missed the point.

The problem of homosexuality is similar. We have too often decried what we call "their choice" as shameful and condemn them to hell. We need first to reflect the Father's love, explain what Jesus did for them, and help them see the hope of a new and wonderful identity without shame. If they make the choice to receive this Gospel, then we can help walk them through transformation of the mind by walking in the Spirit as explained above.

THE FLINTSTONES

As I said in my opening chapter, when I received Christ I attended a church where I was taught a mixture of law and grace. When I felt conviction for lacking the fruit of the Spirit, I would try to do better—of course, with the help of the Holy Spirit, or so I thought. As a result, I became like the Israelites trying to perform the law to please God. I thought I was placing my trust in His grace, but I was, in fact, striving to be the engine that powers my own life.

Folks, the Holy Spirit was sent to be—and desires to be—the engine driving our lives.

Older readers will recall the TV cartoon series of a stone-age family who had vehicles without engines. The show began with an invitation to "Meet the Flintstones!" They pushed their cars around with their feet through the car floor. So many of us live like that today. We invite the Holy Spirit into our vehicle and place Him in the passenger seat. We ask for directions from time to time (only if we are really lost) and occasionally look to Him for approval. However, we're still pushing the vehicle with our own strength.

Folks, the Holy Spirit was sent to be—and desires to be—the engine driving our lives.

If you are a church leader, I pray you will be humble and openhearted enough not to get defensive if you have been teaching law instead of the really Good News of the Father's amazing love and grace. I do not profess to understand all things or to be always right; however, I believe what I have presented here is both backed by Scripture and aligns with the God I have come to know personally. It has also made clear the wonderful identity He has given to me.

As I've said throughout this book, the Scriptures are so often written in a way that cloaks the message. If we are determined to read them with a religious mind, we will be led by the letter of the law and miss God's loving and liberating message. That is why it is critical we depend on the Holy Spirit to lead us into His understanding which always points to sonship. "For as many as are led by the Spirit of God, these are the sons of God." (Romans 8:14, NKJV)

Chapter 12

CHAIN MAIL

We are in a spiritual battle. It's a battle of two Kingdoms—the Kingdom of darkness and God's Kingdom of light—happening both in the spirit realm and on earth. We are in this battle whether we choose to acknowledge it or not. Its epicenter is in the human mind.

I have spent considerable time throughout this book pointing out two very real and serious challenges we each face to being well-equipped to overcome and win this battle. One challenge is the ability to decipher the mysteries of God. As I said before, we have been led to believe that, as Christians, these mysteries have been revealed to us, so we already all know them. I am sorry to say that this simply is not true. They have been made available to us, but we do not necessarily know them.

As we saw earlier, Jesus intentionally kept many things as mysteries and purposefully spoke in parables to the very Israelites He came to reach. (John 1:11-12) One of the problems with not understanding the mysteries is that we do not merely believe *nothing.* In fact, we will believe *something else* until our eyes are opened to the truth. That is where the second serious challenge comes from.

The enemy knows how the flesh operates. He understands our natural gravitation to religious thinking. In an effort to thwart God's revelation, he has developed a very powerful network of deceptions, distorting truth and Scripture to spin a completely different and convincing meaning. I call his deceptive network of lies *chain mail.*

As I explained in chapter 1, chain mail is armor made of many small and strong metal rings linked together into a flexible, protective garment. It was worn by soldiers and knights in medieval times to protect vital organs from being penetrated by a sword or arrow. Each little ring by itself appears insignificant, but together they form an almost impenetrable shield.

Satan's chain mail is designed to block our spiritual hearts from the sword of the Spirit (truth) penetrating our religious minds and revealing God's wonderful mysteries and our true identities—both His and ours.

Countless Scripture passages have been taught with just enough of a deceptive twist to them that, instead of them being encouraging and empowering, now make you feel overwhelmed or heavy with condemnation. These distortions also work to construct a distorted identity resulting in a weakening of our faith.

The following image is an optical illusion of sorts, often used to demonstrate how one image can be viewed completely differently by two different people:

As you observe the image above, you likely see either the head of a young woman as if you are looking at her from her left side as she turns her head away from you, or you see the left profile of the face of an old witch-like woman with her chin jutting outward. (Hint: Most of the young woman's facial profile and chin form the old woman's nose.)

This illusion demonstrates the challenge we each face when discerning the Scriptures. The enemy seeks to greatly influence what we perceive as the truth and wages battle in our minds. That is why Romans 12:1 says we must be transformed by the renewing of our minds. But be encouraged. The more truth is revealed, the more it snowballs into more revelation. The more we focus on the young woman in the image, the more easily we see her when flashing back to look at the image, and the less likely we will be to see the older witch-like woman.

This chapter is devoted to giving just a few examples of Scripture that are typically interpreted through a performance-based religious mindset that subtly distorts what the Spirit desires us to understand. I call these *Chain Mail Examples*. My hope is that they will help to give you a kickstart to viewing Scripture through a more discerning and pure heart, uncontaminated with religious filters.

CHAIN MAIL EXAMPLE #1

I begin with an example that deals with the foundation for understanding the real meaning of the Scriptures. In what we commonly call the Sermon on the Mount, Jesus said, "Blessed are the pure in heart, for they shall see God." (Matthew 5:8 NKJV) Upon reading this verse, many of us feel we fall short. We consciously or subconsciously examine our hearts for things like bitterness, unforgiveness, guile, envy, and many such things. We know we are not perfect and may even feel convicted of a particular issue. *Does this mean I will not see God? In what way will I not see God?* I have even heard some ask, *Could I be lost?*

That little religious voice of accusation whispers into our minds, *I need to do better, I'm disappointing to God,* etc. By lies and subtle condemnation, the spirit of religion will always push us either to distance ourselves from intimacy with the Father or to perform better to try to please Him.

As I demonstrated earlier, Jesus intentionally kept many things away from those whose hearts were not pure. One such example is found in Matthew 13 when Jesus was explaining why He spoke in parables. I will use The Passion Translation, as I find it explains the core issue quite clearly:

> You (the disciples) have been given the intimate experience of insight into the hidden truths and mysteries of the realm of heaven's Kingdom, but they have not. For everyone who listens with an open heart will receive progressively more revelation until he has more than enough. But those who don't listen with an open, teachable heart, even the understanding they think they have will be taken from them. That's why I teach the people using parables, because they think they are looking for truth, yet because their hearts are unteachable, they never discover it. Although they will listen to Me, they never fully perceive the message I speak. (Matthew 13: 11-13 TPT)

The heart God is looking for is genuinely looking for truth. It is receptive to it, even if it rocks existing theology or has costly consequences. Many have become dull to the truth because of religious pride or fear of going against the crowd. Many find it too easy to simply accept salvation and sonship purely by faith and only faith. Such people can only see a God that needs to be pleased with striving for holiness and acceptance. They may say they believe the true Gospel, but there is always a "but".

When I look at this first chain mail example in Matthew 5:8 regarding a pure heart, here is my personal interpretation:

Blessed and fortunate are those whose hearts are not contaminated with religious thinking, pride, fear, or deception, for they will discover God as He really is, not the sin-conscious, religious god Satan wants us to see.

CHAIN MAIL EXAMPLE #2

"God wants to build character." How many times in your Christian life have you heard that statement? Is God interested in character? Of course He is. But not in quite the same way the enemy wants us to focus on it. We love to say God wants to build character. Romans 5:1-5 appears to confirm that God is focused primarily on building character. However, this character is not quite in the way the religious mind perceives it:

> And not only that, but we also glory in tribulation, knowing that tribulation produces perseverance; and perseverance, character; and character, hope. Now hope does not disappoint, because the love of God has been poured out in our hearts by the Holy Spirit who was given to us. (Romans 5:3-5 NKJV)

First, these character attributes are actually the fruit of the Spirit. John 15:3-4 shows that fruit will be born when the branches remain connected to the vine (in relationship and restful trust). Have you ever seen a tree sweat and toil to bear fruit? As we rest and remain in all that Jesus did and walk in confident fellowship with Him and the Father, we naturally will lose the desire to walk in the flesh driven by fear. In that place of love and absence of fear-driven activity, the fruit appears by the grace and power of His life in us.

Romans 5:3-5 seems to progress from character trait to character trait until hope is produced. On the surface, using religious thinking, this really does not make much sense. How could hope develop from perseverance? But here is how I have come to understand this.

When we first read God's Word of truth, we come to a limited understanding that is often not very deep until that belief is truly tested. When tribulation comes, we find ourselves at a crossroads. We are challenged to dig deeper into what the Word says in contradiction to the circumstances we are experiencing, particularly regarding His love towards us, or to fall back on the lies and circumstances that threaten the truth. When that happens, it is like the birds coming to steal the seeds that fell on shallow ground, as described in the parable of the sower. (Matthew 13:18)

As we process surface knowledge into deeper revelatory beliefs, perseverance is produced. As we determine to stand on faith in what the Word says about God, us, and the truth, perseverance develops. At this stage, we grasp deeper meaning and revelation that could not be understood without having to apply it during a time of tribulation. It is no longer head knowledge, but faith that has become part of our character. With this deeper character of faith, resolve, and confidence, a more solid hope is produced because we are more deeply settled in His unwavering love. Our hope becomes firm.

In God's eyes, you are already like Jesus by faith in His grace. What He wants is for you to believe it, to have that same mind of Christ and rest in the fact and reality that you are His perfect child.

My friend, God wants you to be like Jesus, but not in the way most understand that to mean. Jesus understood His identity and was in a deep, confident, and intimate relationship with His Father. He was in complete peace and rest and knew the authority this provided.

In God's eyes, you are already like Jesus by faith in His grace. What He wants is for you to believe it, to have that same mind of Christ and rest in the fact and reality that you are His perfect child. This awareness is the shortest path to be like Jesus because it removes the fears and desires to walk in the flesh. The enemy wants to hide that reality from you and twist it to mean, *If only you could be more like Jesus—but you kinda suck.*

CHAIN MAIL EXAMPLE #3

Throughout the Bible, we see the words *command* and *commandments* used. I've seen many believers struggle with the seemingly harsh and demanding sound of these words. In some instances, Jesus sounds like an encouraging teacher in the first half of a sentence and, in the latter half, seems demanding and unloving. We know obedience is required and appropriate for obvious reasons—it is necessary and critical for our own good and the good of His Kingdom. Obedience is the natural behavior towards someone who loves you and has authority over you. But to demand obedience with a threat of withholding love seems inconsistent with what we have already come to understand about Jesus and the Father. Obviously, God loves obedience. He deserves it because He is God, the ultimate authority over our lives, and has our best interest at heart.

Yet still, we struggle. Let's look at some verses with examples:

- "If you keep My commandments, you will abide in My love, just as I have kept My Father's commandments and abide in His love." (John 15:10 NKJV)

- "You are My friends if you do whatever I command you." (John 15:14 NKJV)

In our English translations, we use the same word *command* or *commandment* for more than seven different Hebrew or Greek words. Each word in these languages has a different meaning, but in English, the same word often gets used to translate them. In modern English, the word *command* usually refers to an authoritative order or demand as used in the military. It is usually associated with domination. Some of the Hebrew and Greek words throughout the Bible refer to giving someone a charge or command in relation to laws and statutes. Like we say today, "Just do it!" In other instances, the word used refers to commanding a demon to come out with authority. The words Jesus used in the verses above were translated from the Greek words that are transliterated as *entellomahee* and *entolay*:

- *Entellomahee:* To charge, to enjoin, instruct, urge; prescribe an action or attitude to be performed or adopted.
- *Entolay:* Authoritative prescription, precept.

Considering all that has been addressed in the previous chapters, we should be understanding that neither Jesus nor the Father is the negatively authoritative, demanding type, even though They hold all authority and power. In light of this, the words *commands* and *commandments* in the verses above are not demands coming from a military type of authority, but more of instruction coming from one who is a loving authority over you as well as the greatest authority on the subject.

It is more like a parent who has authority over their children. The parent expects the child to understand and appreciate that their instructions come from one with wisdom who loves and desires to protect them, lead them into proper development and prosperity. It is proper and expected that a child will obey such instructions out of respect for the position of a parent as well as faith in their motives—the well-being of the child.

It's also more like a doctor who is an authority in medicine prescribing a remedy, than a drill sergeant giving an order and caring nothing about what you think. "Just do it! It's an order!" Of course, Jesus is our Lord, King, and God. Everything He says carries the greatest weight, but it also carries the greatest motive for our good. God through Isaiah gives a good example of motives behind the commandments: "Oh, that you had heeded My commandments! Then your peace would have been like a river, and your righteousness like the waves of the sea." (Isaiah 48:18 NKJV)

In my example above in John 15:10, Jesus is not saying He will love you *if* you keep His commandments. Such an understanding would mean His love is conditional on your performance. He is saying that if we understand the difference between the New Covenant and the Old and follow all that He taught about sonship, we would naturally and confidently remain in His love instead of drifting away. It speaks to a result, not a reward. When we drift back into the ways of religious performance, we are the ones who do not abide or remain in His love. It's not Him kicking us out. Remember, 1 John 4:18 speaks of God's perfect love that drives out all fear of punishment because it is freely given when we were adopted as His children. This truth is further confirmed in 1 John 2:5 NKJV: "But whoever keeps His word, truly the love of God is perfected in him. By this we know that we are in Him."

Religious thinking understands that verse to mean, if we live right (perform well), He will fully love us. This is typical Satanic chain mail crafted by lies and distortion. In reality, John is saying when we remain in the grace and truth of His Gospel, the full love of the Father becomes a deep-seated revelation within our hearts. We will then know this love in a personal and unshakable way.

Neither His love nor friendship is given on the condition of keeping rules and commands. Those are the natural benefits we will experience if we walk in the Spirit, in our true secure identity as His child with a new spirit.

Lastly, obeying His commandment cannot provide salvation any more than disobeying condemns to hell. Salvation is available only by faith in trusting that Jesus (the only acceptable sacrificial Lamb) paid the required price for us. Therefore, a person who has not received Christ nor submitted to His Lordship remains in a lost state regardless of his efforts to obey commandments. The following two verses explain this clearly:

- "For by grace you have been saved through faith, and that not of yourselves, it is the gift of God, not of works, lest anyone should boast." (Ephesians 2:8, NKJV)

- "He who believes in the Son has everlasting life; and he who does not believe the Son shall not see life, but the wrath of God abides on him." (John 3:36, NKJV)

The commandments referred to in the New Testament under the new covenant are given for those who are already saved and are now God's children and should be viewed within that context.

CHAIN MAIL EXAMPLE #4

Jesus won't return until His bride is spotless. I've often heard that statement in churches. It is usually followed with something along the lines of His return being far off because of the poor state of the Church at present. By *poor state*, the speaker usually implies that there is too much sin, poor character, or disunity. This statement does not line up with the real message of the Gospel and all of the scriptural evidence I have been revealing in this book. Thus, it makes a good chain mail example.

Let's look at the Scriptures: "Christ also loved the church and gave Himself for her, that He might sanctify and cleanse her with the washing of water by the word, that He might present her to Himself a glorious church, not having a spot or wrinkle or any such thing, but that she should be holy and without blemish." (Ephesians 5: 25-27 NKJV)

The idea that the church has yet to become spotless and Christ won't return until she does comes from the same deceptive religious thinking. If that statement is true, then Jesus will never be able to return—ever! The whole Gospel is based on the fact that by faith and only faith in what Jesus did to make us sinless, will we ever be considered righteous and pure in the sight of God. He has already done it! The idea that we have to do better or else He can't return is clearly promoting a performance-based Gospel.

The idea that the church has yet to become spotless and Christ won't return until she does comes from the same deceptive religious thinking

If we consider all that was discussed to this point, it is undeniable that when we accept Jesus' sacrifice for our sins, we become born again with a new spirit and are *now* sinless and given the *full* righteousness of God. We have instantly become a child of God, loved as Jesus is loved. If there is anything that Jesus is waiting for, it is for the Church to walk in their full identity, understanding what they already have and accepting it with confidence and simple faith.

We are already spotless and without blemish! As I explained earlier, we know we are made spotless and endued with His righteousness, not only by what the Scriptures clearly explain but also by the sheer fact that He can dwell in us. We have each become the Holy of Holies.

I recently read a statement from someone who said Christ was not ready to return because the Church lacks love. I agree with that statement, but from this angle: When we grasp how simple and free the whole Gospel is, we will personally *know* the love of the Father *on a daily basis*. Honestly, what the Church so lacks is full understanding of God's love towards us. When we do grasp it,

The unsaved can smell religion from afar, and they are repulsed by it, but they cannot easily reject genuine love from the Father.

we will not focus on just saving souls but rather seeking to reconcile them to the Father by *reflecting* the love we have come to deeply understand and know firsthand.

This is what Jesus meant when He said, "Unless we become like little children...." It's all about truly becoming the sons and daughters of God. It is by reflecting the love we know and experience that the lost will be attracted to more than anything else—*"the revealing of the sons of God."* The unsaved can smell religion from afar, and they are repulsed by it, but they cannot easily reject genuine love from the Father.

With these few examples, it is my hope that as you read the Word on your own, you will begin to see countless passages of Scripture that the enemy has distorted for use in his deceptive chain mail. My prayer is that your eyes will be opened more and more to His liberating truth. The more your eyes are opened to who God really is and His perspectives, the more you will see the *beautiful young woman* instead of the *witchlike old lady*.

Then He said to them, "Be diligent to understand the meaning behind everything you hear, for as you do, more understanding will be given to you. And according to the depth of your longing to understand, much more will be added to you. For those who listen with open hearts will receive more revelation. But those who don't listen with open hearts will lose what little they think they have." (Mark 4:24-25 TPT)

Chapter 13

MOVING FORWARD

Mark Twain once inspired a common quotation in publishing, "You don't finish a book; you just publish it." I've certainly found that to be true and discovered that the final chapter is the most challenging. Do I reiterate the key points? Do I try to give direction going forward? Do I develop a study guide with questions and answers to work through?

As I sought direction from the Holy Spirit, I feel peace that I have said all that I need to say at this point. There is no perfectly-finished book, particularly when it addresses controversial issues. It is not my desire to try to lead you beyond this point into how you need to think. It is my hope that I have been a faithful ambassador of reconciliation and have led you to our Father. From this point onward, you will need to intentionally walk this out with Him.

This book is not only about improving your personal life, but also about releasing you into your full destiny with power and authority to bring heaven to Earth. For the last five years, I have been feeling a strong sense that we are at the beginning of a reformation. Reformation does not come from tweaking what exists. It requires a transformation of our minds and hearts, leading to significant change in our actions.

We are in a time when *everything* is being shaken, whether we like it or not. 2020 was a year like no other, and we have found ourselves in a massive spiritual battle against dark forces that seek to transform America into something very contrary to its founding principles.

This is not merely an American issue. We are on the verge of a global tipping point. Clearly, God's Church has not gained dominion over the earth. We have lost sight and understanding of why He said to pray that His Kingdom comes on earth as it is in heaven. America was built on a solid foundation of biblical principles and a deep faith in God. I am not denying that many grave mistakes and injustices have blotted its history, but its founding principles, which I'm certain were inspired by God, have been a guiding beacon for centuries.

As I mentioned in my introduction, an atheistic new world order (or globalization, as some call it) is Satan's ultimate agenda. His goal is to remove God completely and replace Him with the state. It is a system where we become completely dependent on the state—by force. The state decides moral values and what you can and cannot do or have, all under the false premise of seeking equality. In the communist countries where statism exists, most of the world's worst atrocities recorded in modern history have been committed. It is also common knowledge that their citizens have been severely oppressed.

Global statism cannot happen with a strong America firmly standing on its foundations. America has stood for freedom above all other nations. God is a God of freedom. The protector of Christianity and freedom must first be destroyed and removed out of the way for this one-world system to be implemented as foretold in the Book of Revelation. Antichrist forces have been working for decades to dismantle our Judeo-Christian foundations and have climbed to the top of the pillars of society that form our culture in order to reshape it. These "seven mountains" of culture, as I have already referred to, are government, education, religion, business, media, arts and entertainment, and the family. God's people have believed the lie that most of these areas are secular and should be left for the secular world, only to find ourselves becoming a subculture struggling to keep our freedoms.

The Church has to awaken to these realities. These areas must be regained, or life as we know it could be permanently lost. Whatever strategy is to be implemented needs to be carried out by a Church that is far more powerful and effective than the one that has existed for the last few decades. The Church needs first to be reformed through a deeper understanding of its true identity and its Kingdom-building mission on Earth—from God's perspective. I ask with all seriousness: how willing are we to walk away from all that we have built and allow the Spirit to hand us a new blueprint?

There are a number of aspects to this reformation that when pieced together will result in the greatest end-time move of God, like nothing the world has ever seen. One aspect will be the Church moving outside the walls of the church buildings with a clear understanding that the pursuit of these cultural pillars is very much a Kingdom pursuit.

I did not spend much time on this particular aspect, as I believe I have been assigned to a specific area on which to focus. It is the area that moves us from living as fearful, weak servants to bold, confident children operating in power and authority. It will take believers who are living outside of the institutional boxes of religious thought. These are people who do not seek to get credit for anything nor to be called anything. They have no desire to build something of their own. They desire only to hear their Father's voice and allow His Spirit to guide them into new areas with a fearless faith and confidence that can only come through a real understanding of their true purpose and identity. Without this deeper change in the hearts and minds of God's people, we will continue to fail in our quest for Kingdom dominion on the Earth.

It is basic common knowledge that Satan's number-one weapon is fear. We have sought to manage it enough to continue with life as normal. However, his recent onslaught is opening the Church's eyes to its fears. The old fear-management techniques are not working. Sadly, one of the main sources of fear is false religious systems. That is why God is disrupting them and setting the prisoners free.

NEW WINESKINS

Are we fighting to stabilize the "same old, same old" and get back to our comfort zones? Do you really believe this is the best the Church of Jesus Christ can do? If that's where we are, we have settled for Satan's chain mail of distortions and lies, willing to remain as "good servants" just trying to get by. I am certain that anyone wanting to hold onto such a mindset will be left behind to dwell in religious mediocrity.

My friend, we are in a season of life-changing paradigm shifts for many. It's about God working to do a new thing in us and through us. "Behold, I will do a new thing, Now it shall come forth; Shall you not know it?" (Isaiah 43:19a NKJV)

Let me share a personal experience parallel to where I believe many in the Church are today. As I write, I am very much in the midst of a metamorphosis of my business if we are going to survive the ravages of COVID-19. I have experienced extensive losses after forty-seven years of a challenging but successful business. A huge portion of the value of the business evaporated almost overnight. What we have been left with has to be carefully managed in order to stay afloat and reshape the business in a fast-changing environment. Over the last two years, a number of our locations were beautifully remodeled at extensive cost, but we have come to the clear conclusion that we need to drastically change our model. Our stores need to be smaller and more efficient. We must develop a more competitive model to compete with the online budget stores, or we will completely cease to exist.

In order to move from a cumbersome caterpillar to a light butterfly that can fly and reach new heights, we have to be willing to walk away from all of the money, time, and effort spent on the former model. We have to be prepared to walk away from what we are comfortable with and intentionally step into what is *needed*. That is a very difficult thing to do, but it is necessary in order to experience what God really has in store for us.

Some of my stores are beautiful *caterpillars* created by many hours of fine workmanship at considerable investment. We will have to change them if we want to survive in spite of the loss incurred. Likewise, we can never see the new thing God wants to do if we hold on to our old paradigms, positions, ministries, egos, or our treasured reputations.

A MIND OF YOUR OWN

One of my favorite Bible characters is Balaam's donkey. Yes, I said Balaam's (talking) donkey in Numbers 22: 21-39. There are many biblical characters I have identified with over the years, but that donkey is where I am at today. It does not matter to me how many millions of people are moving in a certain direction. If I feel disturbed in my spirit, I am digging in my heels and will not hop onto the train. Life is too short. I got off the train a long time ago. When we go in the wrong direction, we will end up at the wrong destination (like the train station vision in chapter 8). At that point, it makes no difference if millions are with you; it's still the wrong destination with circumstances God never intended for you. Even worse, it may be too late to go back.

God wants to stop the hamster wheels and is using the pandemic disruptions and other current events to do so. He is speaking to us, but we have to have spiritually sensitive ears to hear. Misaligned busyness dulls our ability to receive new revelation and direction.

It is my hope that if you are not already comfortably hearing your Father's voice that you will begin to hear Him daily. He is your Father and desires to be in constant communication with you directly. Many Christians are taught not to expect this or taught that He speaks only through the Bible. Many of us are also led to believe that He speaks primarily through leaders. That is certainly not the truth, as I explained earlier.

God speaks in so many ways that you cannot count them. It is time for His children to learn to listen to His voice for themselves. While I did share with you at the beginning some of the many ways God clearly spoke to me, I did not get into teaching on the many ways God speaks because it is not my focus or calling. If you really want to understand more on this topic, I would recommend you read Lana Vawser's book titled *The Prophetic Voice of God*. There is also an interesting and beautiful song by Dante Bowe called *The Voice of God*. I strongly recommend you listen to it, as well. These will get you started on the right track.

BEYOND REDEMPTION

The revival I believe we are about to see will come through sons and daughters that do not merely preach salvation but actually lead the lost to their Father. They will help bridge people into the rest and confidence that only a child can experience. Jesus said, "He who has seen Me has seen the Father." (John 14:9) We are Jesus' Body and must reflect *the Father* as Jesus did. This reflection is what will be most attractive to the world and touch the hearts of the lost.

The revival I believe we are about to see will come through sons and daughters that do not merely preach salvation but actually lead the lost to their Father.

When Billy Graham died, I heard a reporter on the news say, "His message was all about redemption!" Not quite, but the redemption message is what most of the world has heard from the Church. It speaks mainly to God's love saving us from eternal damnation. While on road trips, I have seen countless signs on highways with the words "Jesus Saves!" True, but it's only half the message.

I have come to realize that many things we thought were unique to Jesus do also apply to us as His Body here on Earth. As I just explained, reflecting and revealing the Father is one, and *reconciliation* is another. As it was for Jesus, reconciliation is also our primary mission and ministry. Our focus and end is not the salvation of souls, but ultimately to lead these saved souls into God's family through the Good News of reconciliation (recall Jesus' focus in the parable of the prodigal son).

The following Scriptures reveal this quite clearly:

Now all things are of God, who reconciled us to Himself through Jesus Christ, and has given us the ministry of reconciliation, that is, that God was in Christ reconciling the world to Himself...

Now then, we are ambassadors for Christ, as though God were pleading through us: we implore you on Christ's behalf, be reconciled to God. (2 Corinthians 5:18 & 20 NKJV)

Everything that I have written in this book is intended to help you make a major, life-altering paradigm shift into understanding the mysteries of God and Satan's chain mail of religious distortion.

I reiterate that one of the biggest problems and most challenging concepts to explain is that many of us are so taught and programmed to *only* think Jesus. We never come to understand how to truly live daily as the Father's sons and daughters. However, it is this truth that opens the door to full Kingdom living. I think Satan knows he would fail miserably trying to downplay Jesus, so he works diligently and effectively to keep us focused solely on Jesus and not the other half of the Gospel. As a result, we primarily focus on Jesus while the Gospels show undeniably that Jesus came to open the door to our Father and demonstrate how to live in relationship with the Father. Jesus constantly points us to our Father.

Before you jump to the conclusion that I see Jesus as someone you meet in passing and move on, that is neither what I have said throughout this book nor what I am saying now. Without following Jesus and abiding in Him (in the manner revealed in the Scriptures), we can do nothing! He is our Lord and the Second Person in the Godhead. He is the Alpha and Omega through whom all things were made, and the One who leads us victoriously into the culmination of the ages as described in the Book of Revelation. He deserves our neverending praise and all glory.

But do you think Jesus is pleased when we do not want to fully embrace why He came and what He knows is best for us and His Kingdom? I am not saying to reduce or remove any aspect of your relationship with Jesus. It is all critically necessary and wonderful! The problem that exists throughout the Church is that we more or less stay at the door to the Father's house. We need the other half of the equation to see everything clearly. It is what the whole of creation is eagerly awaiting. "For the earnest expectation of the creation eagerly awaits for the revealing of the sons of God." (Romans 8: 19 NKJV) Jesus Himself said, "But the hour is coming, and now is, when the true worshipers will worship the Father in spirit and in truth; for the Father is seeking such to worship Him." (John 4:23 NKJV) I encourage you to listen to the song "Home" by Dante Bowe.

I conclude with Jesus' words again as He was ending His prayer in John 17: "I have revealed to them who you are and will continue to make you even more real to them, so that they may experience the same endless love that you have for Me, for your love will now live in them, even as I live in them." (John 17:26 TPT)

Thank you for allowing me to share my heart with you.

ABOUT THE AUTHOR

Colin Ferreira considers himself a regular and practical guy. He is a businessman and the owner of a leading chain of optical stores in Trinidad and Tobago but presently lives in Georgia, U.S.A. For most of his Christian life, he was a senior leader in the churches he attended. However, his passion to see the relevance of God in business led him on a path of experiences that would launch him as a pioneer and leader in the area of marketplace ministry in the Caribbean region and beyond. Unexpectedly, his quest to see God as He truly is, thrust him suddenly onto a completely different and challenging path that resulted in this book and a much clearer sense of purpose. He is also very happily married and is the father of nine children presently between the ages of 26 and 8.

ACKNOWLEDGMENTS

To my wife Cheryl: The journey that led to this book was during one of the darkest and most challenging times in my life. During this period of what felt like deep darkness and confusion, I know I was at times a difficult person to live with. When I asked God to send me the wife that was best for me, He faithfully answered my prayer. I am certain that I would not have survived, far less completed, this work without you by my side as a pillar of support and affirmation as well as an excellent sounding board. This has not been *my* journey but *our* journey. Thank you, my Love!

My very dear friends Jim and Jolene Walker whom God brought into my life for such a time as this. You have been such encouragers and a blessing! Thank you for your genuine support!

Made in the USA
Columbia, SC
17 April 2021